frugal
FEASTS

CHRISTINE McFADDEN

B XTREE

PUBLISHED IN ASSOCIATION WITH
HEALTHY EATING MAGAZINE

ACKNOWLEDGEMENTS

I would like to thank Mary Kennedy and Jane Last of
Healthy Eating magazine, and Penny Simpson
and Susanna Wadeson of Boxtree for their
help in bringing about the publication of this book.
I am also grateful to my husband, Ed, and long-standing
friends Anna and Alex, for their support and
enthusiasm during the recipe testing.

First published in Great Britain in 1996 by Boxtree Limited.

Text © Mediawatch Ltd/Christine McFadden 1996
Photographs © Gary Calloway 1996

1 2 3 4 5 6 7 8 9 10

Jacket and text designed by Sarah Hall
Printed and bound in Great Britain by Cox and Wyman Ltd,
Reading, Berkshire for

Boxtree Limited
Broadwall House
21 Broadwall
London SE1 9PL

A CIP catalogue entry for this book is available from the
British Library

ISBN 0 7522 1027 0

Front and back cover photographs by © Gary Calloway

CONTENTS

INTRODUCTION

The eighteen months spent writing *Frugal Feasts* was a time of deep financial challenge for my husband and me, but it was also a time of great enjoyment in the kitchen. We suddenly lost nearly half our regular family income and, both being self-employed, we were finding the recession an uncomfortably rocky ride. Cooking became a more relaxed and spontaneous affair as I began to find ways of drastically cutting the food bill without resorting to boring meals.

I started to grow herbs and unusual salad leaves and vegetables in our small urban garden. The satisfaction of picking my own rocket and radicchio instead of paying supermarket prices was immense. I even managed to grow chillies, lemon grass and Mexican tomatillos. More importantly, I found gardening a wonderful way of calming down during periods of prolonged stress.

I got to know allotment owners, local greengrocers, butchers and market stall holders, and learned to restrict supermarket visits to the end of the day when there were likely to be bargains. I developed an eagle eye for prices and became wise to what I call supermarket tricks – like selling prepackaged fruit and vegetables and charging more for it than the same produce sold loose, then charging a lower price the next week. I never went shopping without a notebook and calculator.

Menus and shopping lists became flexible, as all sorts of free goodies seemed to come our way. Sometimes it might be a whole large trout from a neighbourly fishing enthusiast, or a bag of earthy parsnips from the greengrocer, or golden quinces from a friend's tree. Whatever we were given, a meal could be created around it.

I built up a storecupboard of weird and wonderful spices, sauces and condiments which became essential for spiking up cheap, bland ingredients such as pulses and grains. Whenever there was any spare cash or birthday money, I indulged in a bottle of good olive oil or some such culinary treat.

Cooking for friends has always been one of my biggest pleasures. In the past, this had tended to be a somewhat lavish affair, but I found our frugal feasts every bit as enjoyable – if not more so. I hope you will enjoy them too.

The book shows two vegetarian and two non-vegetarian seasonal menus per month from January through to December. I've allowed a maximum budget of £1.75 a head for three courses based on the cheapest ingredients available at that time. Dishes from the chapter on accompanying vegetables are included in the total cost of the menu. The budget does not include wine, but let's assume your guests will bring a bottle or two.

FRUGAL STRATEGIES

There's no doubt that entertaining on a restricted budget needs careful planning, but it also means being an opportunist. If you come across a bargain, make the most of it and re-think your menu. That way your cooking won't get stuck in a rut and you still won't break the bank.

Creative shopping skills are essential for creative frugal feasts. It's a good idea to go armed with a list as in that way unnecessary items won't find their way into your supermarket trolley. But at the same time be flexible; watch out for supermarket special offers and snap them up, either to cook now or for freezing. Produce coming to the end of its season is generally cheaper, as are perishables which have reached their sell-by date.

Supermarkets are very clever with their pricing methods. You'll often see the same stuff differently packaged and differently priced. For instance, identical apples could be sold at £1.19 for a kilogram pack, or loose at 39p a pound. The kilogram pack looks like a bargain, but in fact is 13p a pound more expensive. So take a calculator and check prices and weights. Better still, keep your local market or greengrocer in business and look for bargains there. My local market sells spinach at 69p/lb (supermarket £1.30), shallots at 55p/lb (supermarket £1.30) and pork knuckle at an unbelievable 73p/lb (supermarket £1.29). Cheap cuts of meat like this make wonderful stews with rich lip-smacking gravy.

Don't look down on frozen meat as it is always cheaper than fresh; give it tender loving care by way of zesty marinades and leisurely cooking. However, don't be seduced, as I was, by cheap bags of frozen chicken 'portions' (as opposed to 'quarters'). Supermarkets are very cunning – what appeared to be meaty-looking chicken turned out to be portions from the parson's nose end with a huge flap of fatty skin neatly folded out of sight and hardly any meat.

Rigorous portion control is another skill for successful frugal feasting. Work out exactly how much rice or pasta you need to feed four people and then cook exactly that. People often eat less of these fillers than you would expect. If you're worried about portions looking mean, use a smaller serving bowl and pile it high.

Present your feasts imaginatively. Use your most colourful bowls and plates. If you can't afford flowers on the table, a jugful of leafy herbs, wild flowers, or even weeds and grasses looks just as good, if not better. Garnishing the most mundane of dishes with a scattering of chopped herbs or nuts, a swirl of yogurt, or a sliver of lime always makes the food look more appetizing, and shows that you've enjoyed cooking it too.

STOCKING UP

A judiciously stocked storecupboard and freezer are the key to successful frugal feasting. Even the most bland and boring food can be brought to life by the imaginative use of spices, bottled sauces and condiments: they are well worth the investment. The following may sound a lot, but you don't have to buy all the items at once, and many you will already have.

STORECUPBOARD

Oils, vinegars and seasonings
Light olive oil
Extra virgin olive oil
Walnut oil
Sunflower oil
Groundnut oil
Wine vinegar
Balsamic vinegar
Japanese soy sauce
Harissa sauce
Dijon mustard

Herbs and spices
Cumin seeds
Coriander seeds
Cardamom pods
Cloves
Cinnamon sticks
Paprika
Cayenne
Vanilla pods
Dried oregano and thyme
Bay leaves
Dried chilli flakes
Coarse sea salt flakes
Black peppercorns
Dried green peppercorns

Noodles, grains and pulses
Dried pasta (Italian brands are best)
Rice
Bulgar wheat
Egg noodles
Couscous
Polenta
Black turtle beans
Kidney beans
Haricot beans
Butter beans
Flageolet beans
Chick-peas
Puy lentils

Nuts and seeds
Sesame seeds
Sunflower seeds
Pumpkin seeds
Walnuts
Almonds
Peanuts
Cashews
Pine kernels
Pistachios

Cans and bottles
Chopped tomatoes
Tomato purée
Canned tuna
Sardines
Mackerel fillets
Olives

FREEZER
Ciabatta bread
Pitta bread
Broad beans
Sweetcorn kernels
Spinach
Chicken quarters
New Zealand lamb

GLOSSARY OF INGREDIENTS

Some of the ingredients used in this book may be unfamiliar to you. In most cases a substitute can be used, but it's worth trying to find the more obscure items so that you can experience new tastes and expand your cooking repertoire. Ethnic stores, street markets and the better healthfood stores are rewarding hunting grounds.

CHILLIES

I simply could not manage without chillies. I don't necessarily use them in melt-down curries, but to add just a touch of colour, flavour and heat here and there, even in fruit salads. I find a small bottle of dried chilli flakes is the cheapest and most convenient way of using them. Fresh chillies are more expensive, but a few go a long way. Always discard the seeds before chopping and afterwards thoroughly wash your hands and utensils. Be especially careful not to touch sensitive areas such as your eyes or mouth, otherwise you'll get chilli burn.

GRAINS

Together with pulses, grains are the frugal feaster's staple. They cost next to nothing, they're filling, energy-giving and nutritious, and can be used in salads, soups, casseroles and vegetable dishes. The most useful to have are rice, bulgar wheat, couscous, whole wheat berries and polenta. Polenta is a bright yellow cornmeal from northern Italy, which cooks like porridge. It has a mild, deeply satisfying flavour and is my number one comfort food.

HERBS

Use fresh herbs whenever possible. The most useful are basil, rosemary, thyme, mint, chives, coriander, and flat-leafed parsley which has a brighter, fresher flavour than ordinary curled parsley. Avoid buying coriander and flat-leafed parsley from supermarkets. They charge the earth for a few measly sprigs and don't seem to have cottoned on to the fact that more and more enterprising greengrocers are selling good-sized bunches for the same price. Ethnic stores have always sold these herbs at reasonable prices. There are many neglected varieties of herbs with beautiful flavours which will transform your cooking. They are worth growing yourself, even in a pot on a window-sill. Try lovage, hyssop, salad burnet or savory. Of the dried herbs, I think only thyme and oregano are worth using. They benefit from dry-frying to bring out the aroma. Simply put the required amount in a small, heavy-based pan without any oil and heat until you smell the aroma.

NUTS AND SEEDS

Nuts and seeds are expensive by weight, but you only need a small quantity at a time. Being a good source of protein, minerals and fat, they come in handy for padding out frugal salads and stews, and adding texture. Sesame, sunflower and pumpkin seeds, walnuts, whole almonds with skin, peanuts, cashews, pine kernels and pistachios are the most useful. Nuts and seeds are a bit cheaper in healthfood stores than in supermarkets. Buy them in small quantities as they soon become rancid. As with dried herbs, the flavour becomes much richer if you dry-fry or toast them first. Dry-fry seeds without any oil in a small, heavy-based pan until they smell fragrant. Put nuts in a single layer in a roasting tin in a preheated oven at 180°C/350°F/Gas 4 for 3-10 minutes until golden. Wrap them in a tea towel and rub briskly to remove the skins.

OILS
Olive oil

It really is worth investing in a bottle of extra virgin olive oil to use in salads. The rich fruity flavour will transform even the most ordinary lettuce leaf. I'm not suggesting you buy one of those really expensive estate-bottled oils, a supermarket oil will be just fine. One tablespoon works out at 13p and is worth every penny. Where I have specified olive oil for cooking, use the cheaper 'pure' olive oil, which is a blend of refined and virgin olive oil.

Nut oils
These are expensive and not strictly essential, but a few drops of hazelnut or walnut oil will lift the most mundane of salads into the realms of gastronomic euphoria. If you're lucky enough to be given a bottle, eke it out by combining it with ordinary olive oil or a neutral oil such as sunflower.

Vegetable oils
The best all-purpose oils for cooking are sunflower oil and groundnut oil. Groundnut oil is ideal for deep-frying and stir-frying as it has a high 'smoke point'. These oils are preferable to corn oil or soy oil, both of which I find rather cloying.

PULSES
Cheap, filling and nutritious, pulses are one of the frugal feaster's staples. Build up a library of colours so that you have, say, pale green flageolets, speckled pink borlottis, glossy black turtle beans and creamy white haricots, and bean dishes will never be boring again. Chick-peas and tiny purply-brown Puy lentils are useful to have too. There are two schools of thought on preparation. Most cooks specify overnight soaking, but some American and Mexican cooks pour scorn on this and cook their beans unsoaked. I have tried both ways and cannot honestly tell the difference. Cooking unsoaked beans means you don't have to plan ahead, but it takes longer. Some dried beans contain a toxin which causes severe stomach upsets and even death. Always boil them rapidly for 15 minutes to destroy the toxin, and then continue to cook in the usual way. Add salt towards the end of cooking time, otherwise the skins become tough.

SALT AND PEPPER
It is worth investing in coarse sea salt flakes. They provide crunchy bursts of flavour and taste quite different from ordinary table salt. Freshly ground black peppercorns are a must too. Dried green peppercorns are another useful item as they have a lovely smoky flavour. A small jar doesn't cost the earth and will last for months.

SOY SAUCE
Soy sauce is an essential item for frugal feasts. It adds a warm flavour to grain dishes and vegetables, and can be used in salad dressings. I prefer the traditionally made Japanese soy sauces, such as shoyu and tamari (wheat-free). They have a mellower flavour than Chinese soy sauce. You can buy them in good healthfood stores and a small bottle will last for weeks.

SPICES
It is always worth having a few spices in the cupboard. They are relatively cheap and are essential for enlivening bland ingredients such as pulses, grains and root vegetables. Buy your spices whole and grind them as you need them: that way they'll taste fresher and you won't need as much. The most useful are coriander, cumin, cardamom, cloves, cinnamon, paprika, cayenne and vanilla. If you enjoy Indian cooking you might want to include mustard seed, garam masala, turmeric and ground fenugreek as well. Another useful one is asafoetida, which you can only buy in ethnic stores. It smells terrible, but when cooked has a lovely warm mellow flavour something like onions and mushrooms – useful to have if you're out of either of these vegetables. As with dried herbs, spices benefit from dry-frying to bring out their flavour.

VINEGAR
Together with extra virgin olive oil, a small bottle of balsamic vinegar is a real 'must have'. Made in Italy from sweet wine, it is highly aromatic so a little goes a long way. One tablespoon works out at 12p. Eke it out by mixing with red wine vinegar. It's useful to have white wine vinegar too. It is lighter than red wine vinegar and goes best with mild-tasting salad greens, whereas red and balsamic vinegars are better with gutsy leaves such as raw spinach.

JANUARY

Traditionally a time of bleakness and regretted resolutions, the weeks following Christmas are in fact one of the better times for the thrifty cook.

It is a relief to return to simpler food after the festivities. There is plenty of fresh produce around at reasonable prices such as winter greens, root vegetables, and citrus fruit. And there are bargains to be had as retailers sell off Christmas fare, such as cranberries, nuts and dried fruit.

The price of meat and poultry is reasonable because of a fall in demand. Frozen turkeys can be had for a song, if you feel you can face another one, but a turkey in the freezer will come in handy at Easter. Game birds are at the end of their season and should be cheap.

Marmalade makers should watch out for Seville oranges as they have a short season at the end of the month. They make good steamed puddings and ice cream, too.

BARGAIN FOOD IN SEASON

Vegetables
Brussels sprouts ● Cabbages ● Kale ● Leeks ● Root vegetables

Fruit
Apples ● Citrus fruit ● Cranberries ● Dried fruit ● Nuts ●
Pears ● Pomegranates

MENU 1
Non-vegetarian
Total cost £6.31

●

**Celery, Apple and
Brazil Nut Salad**

●

**Lamb and Aubergine
Casserole with Roasted Garlic
and Chillies**

●

**Cranberry and Apricot
Compote**

Celery, Apple and Brazil Nut Salad

Cost 77p
Serves 4

This is good for emptying the Christmas nut bowl. If you don't have Brazils, use whatever you have to hand. Toasting the nuts intensifies the flavour.

40 g (1½ oz) shelled Brazil nuts
1 crisp red-skinned apple, unpeeled
squeeze of lemon juice
6 tender celery stalks, cut into thin
diagonal slices
handful of lamb's lettuce or trimmed
watercress

DRESSING
½ tsp Dijon mustard
1 tsp redcurrant or cranberry jelly
1 tsp lemon juice
salt and freshly ground black pepper
3 tbsp extra virgin olive oil

1 Put the Brazil nuts on a baking sheet and toast in a medium-hot oven for 3-5 minutes until golden. Chop roughly.

2 Quarter and core the apple. Slice lengthways into very thin segments. Sprinkle with lemon juice to prevent discolouration.
3 Arrange the apples, celery and lamb's lettuce on individual plates or a serving dish. Sprinkle with the Brazil nuts.
4 Mix the mustard, redcurrant jelly, lemon juice, and salt and pepper until smooth. Whisk in the oil. Spoon the dressing over the salad and serve at once.

Lamb and Aubergine Casserole with Roasted Garlic and Chillies

Cost: £3.31
Serves 4

It is often more economical to buy a cheap cut of lamb with the bone in, such as knuckle or shoulder, and do the trimming yourself (give the bone to the dog or use to make stock). In this case you'll need about 600 g (1¼ lb) including the bone. Cut the meat into really small pieces – that way it goes further. Pad out with rice and chick-peas flavoured with toasted spices, roasted garlic and chilli.

2 large fresh chillies
2 large garlic cloves, unpeeled
1 tsp each coriander and cumin seeds
3 tbsp vegetable oil
450 g (1 lb) boneless stewing lamb,
diced
1 onion, chopped
100 g (4 oz) brown long-grain rice
75 g (3 oz) chick-peas, soaked overnight
and cooked
400 g (14 oz) can chopped tomatoes
1 small aubergine, cubed
100 g (4 oz) green beans, chopped
425-600 ml (¾-1 pt) stock
salt and freshly ground black pepper
3 tbsp chopped fresh coriander
plain yogurt, to serve

1 Roast the chillies and garlic in a preheated oven at 220°C/425°F/Gas 7 for 15 minutes. Remove the skins and seeds from the chillies and the skins from the garlic. Chop the flesh roughly.

2 Dry-fry the coriander and cumin in a small, heavy-based pan until the aroma rises. Crush with a pestle and mortar then mix to a paste with the chillies and garlic.

3 Heat 1 tbsp of oil in a large pan. Brown the lamb and set aside.

4 Heat the remaining oil and gently fry the onion for 5 minutes. Stir in the rice and the chilli paste, and gently fry, stirring, for 3 minutes until the rice is translucent.

5 Add the lamb, chick-peas, tomatoes, aubergine, beans, stock and seasoning. Bring to the boil, then cover and simmer gently for about 1 hour until the lamb is tender. Add a little more stock if necessary. The rice will absorb most of the liquid but the mixture should still be wet.

6 Sprinkle with the coriander and serve with yogurt.

Cranberry and Apricot Compote

Cost: £2.23
Serves 4

Cranberries are really cheap after Christmas. They combine well with dried fruit so you could add leftover raisins to the apricots. If you have any black seedless grapes that need using up, throw these in as well.

**225 g (8 oz) sugar
600 ml (1 pt) water
thinly pared rind of 1 small orange
225 g (8 oz) cranberries**

**1 knob stem ginger, chopped
juice of 1 small orange
175 g (6 oz) dried apricots, quartered
whipped cream, to serve**

1 Put the sugar, water and orange rind in a saucepan. Stir over a medium heat until the sugar has dissolved. Bring to the boil, then boil rapidly for 2 minutes.

2 Fish out the orange peel and add the cranberries to the syrup. Simmer over a very low heat for 5 minutes. Do not allow to boil.

3 Add the stem ginger and orange juice, then pour the mixture over the apricots. Leave to macerate for several hours.

4 Serve chilled with whipped cream.

NUTRITIONAL INFORMATION

First course per portion: calories 170
• protein 2g • fat 16g •
carbohydrate 5g • fibre 2g •
source of: vitamins C, E

Main course per portion: calories 420
• protein 30g • fat 21g •
carbohydrate 32g • fibre 3g •
source of: iron, zinc, B vitamins, fibre

Dessert per portion: calories 320 •
protein 2g • fat 0g • carbohydrate 82g
• fibre 5g • source of: fibre,
vitamin C, beta-carotene

Chilli Bean and Avocado Dip

Cost: £2.05
Serves 4

Roasted garlic and chillies have a lovely mellow flavour. It is worth doing more than you need as they will keep for a few days in the fridge and make lively additions to soups, casseroles and bean dishes. The bean dip can be prepared a day ahead, but the avocado dip should be whizzed up at the last minute – it loses its bright green colour if left hanging around. Serve the dips with toasted fingers of pitta bread.

CHILLI BEAN DIP
100 g (4 oz) kidney beans, unsoaked
1 L (1¾ pt) water
½ onion, roughly chopped
½ tsp salt
2 garlic cloves, unpeeled
1 fat green chilli
juice of 1 lime
freshly ground black pepper
2 tbsp olive oil

AVOCADO DIP
2 avocados
juice of 1 lemon
2 tbsp finely chopped onion
1 tomato, peeled, deseeded and chopped
1 small green chilli, deseeded and chopped
3 tbsp chopped fresh coriander
¼ tsp salt

TO SERVE
1 small lettuce
coriander or parsley sprigs, to garnish
fingers of toast or pitta bread, to serve

1 Put the beans in a small saucepan with the water. Bring to the boil, then boil rapidly for 15 minutes. Reduce the heat a bit, and continue to cook at a lively simmer for 45 minutes, or until the beans are fairly soft. Add the onion and salt, and cook for another 45 minutes until the beans are very soft and the liquid is becoming soupy.

2 Meanwhile put the garlic and chilli in a small roasting tin. Roast in a preheated oven at 180°C/350°F/Gas 4 for 20-25 minutes until the garlic is soft and the chilli is slightly blackened. Remove the skin from the garlic, and skin and seeds from the chilli.

3 Drain the beans, reserving the liquid, and put in a food processor with the garlic, chilli, lime juice, pepper and olive oil. Whizz to a purée, adding some of the bean liquid if necessary. Check the seasoning and add more salt if necessary.

4 To make the avocado dip, put all the ingredients in a food processor and whizz to a chunky purée.

5 Arrange a few lettuce leaves on individual plates. Add a dollop of each dip, garnish with a sprig of coriander and serve with fingers of toast or pitta bread.

Chicken with Spicy Yogurt

Cost: £3.77
Serves 4

Chicken legs are cheap because everybody wants the breasts. Supermarkets sometimes sell bargain packs of drumsticks which are worth snapping up to put in the freezer. But beware of chicken 'portions' – see page 7. Marinate the chicken overnight if possible. Serve with a green vegetable and Oven-Baked Buttered Potatoes (58p, page 120) or rice.

MARINADE
150 ml (¼ pt) set yogurt
2.5 cm (1 in) piece fresh ginger root
50 g (2 oz) onion, cut into small chunks
3 garlic cloves, crushed

1 fresh chilli, deseeded and chopped
½ tsp cumin seeds, crushed
½ tsp salt

900 g (2 lb) chicken drumsticks
3 tbsp vegetable oil
1 onion, chopped
1 red pepper, deseeded and diced
300 ml (½ pt) set yogurt
150 ml (¼ pt) stock or vegetable water
4 tbsp chopped fresh coriander

1 To make the marinade, tip the yogurt into a bowl. Put the ginger in a garlic press and squeeze the juice into the yogurt. Do the same with the onion. Add the debris from the garlic press to the yogurt. Stir in the remaining ingredients, mixing well.

2 Put the drumsticks in a shallow dish. Pour over the marinade, turning the chicken to coat. Cover and leave to marinate in the fridge for at least 3 hours, or overnight.

3 Heat the oil in a large frying pan. Add the onion and red pepper, and gently fry for 5 minutes until softened.

4 Add the chicken and fry over a medium heat for about 20 minutes, turning, until beginning to colour. Stir in a few spoonsful of the yogurt, scraping the sediment at the bottom of the pan. Cover and cook for 40 minutes, gradually adding the rest of the yogurt and turning the chicken so that it cooks evenly.

5 Uncover and raise the heat slightly. Stir in the stock, scraping up all the juices. Simmer for a few minutes more, stirring, until the sauce has thickened slightly. Add the coriander just before serving.

Seville Orange Pudding with Marmalade Sauce

Cost: £1.18
Serves 4

Normally snapped up by marmalade makers, Seville oranges can also make a wonderfully comforting sponge pudding. If you miss their short season use ordinary oranges instead. This is fine with just the sauce, but a blob of double cream would add the finishing touch.

100 g (4 oz) butter
100 g (4 oz) sugar
2 eggs, beaten
100 g (4 oz) self-raising flour
1 tsp baking powder
1 tsp ground cinnamon
pinch of salt
finely grated zest and juice of
2 Seville oranges
4 tbsp breadcrumbs

MARMALADE SAUCE
6 tbsp marmalade
3 tbsp water
1 tbsp brandy (optional)

1 Cream the butter and sugar together until light and fluffy. Gradually add the eggs.

2 Sift together the flour, baking powder, cinnamon and salt. Gradually beat this into the egg mixture, followed by 2 teaspoons of the orange zest and 75 ml (3 fl oz) of the juice. Stir in the breadcrumbs.

3 Pour into a lightly greased 850 ml (1½ pt) pudding basin and cover with greased foil. Stand in a roasting tin of hot water and bake in a preheated oven at 180°C/350°F/Gas 4 for 50-60 minutes until a skewer inserted in the centre comes out clean.

4 To make the sauce, melt the marmalade in a small saucepan with the water and brandy, if using. Simmer for a few minutes.

5 Loosen the pudding with the tip of a knife and turn out on to a serving plate. Pour over a little of the sauce and serve the rest in a small jug.

NUTRITIONAL INFORMATION
First course per portion: calories 225 ● protein 7g ● fat 15g ● carbohydrate 16g ● fibre 6g ● source of: iron, zinc, vitamins B1, B6, C, E, folate

Main course per portion: calories 300 ● protein 28g ● fat 16g ● carbohydrate 13g ● fibre 1g ● source of: calcium, iron, zinc, iodine, vitamins A, B group, C

Dessert per portion: calories 440 ● protein 6g ● fat 24g ● carbohydrate 51g ● fibre 1g ● source of: iron, iodine, vitamins A, E, B group

4 Chop a handful of parsley and set aside. Add
the remaining parsley to the pan. Bring to the
boil, then simmer for 2-3 minutes. The parsley
should still be bright green.
5 Transfer the mixture to a food processor and
liquidize for 3 minutes. Push through a sieve,
pressing with the back of a wooden spoon to
extract as much liquid as possible.
6 Return to the pan. Add the milk, season to
taste and reheat gently. Garnish each serving
with the reserved parsley.

MENU 3
Vegetarian
Total cost £6.63
●
Parsley Soup
●
Fusilli with Roasted Pepper and Olive Sauce
●
Apple and Coriander Crème Brûlée

Parsley Soup

Cost: £1.50
Serves 4

*Parsley stalks usually get thrown away but
here they intensify the flavour of this
deliciously clean-tasting, vitamin-packed
soup. If you can get some free parsley, this
dish will cost next to nothing. You may be
lucky enough to have a fishmonger who still
gives away parsley with the fish.*

175 g (6 oz) parsley
40 g (1½ oz) butter
1 large potato, diced
1 onion, sliced
3 celery stalks, sliced
700 ml (1¼ pt) vegetable stock
150 ml (¼ pt) full-cream milk
salt and freshly ground black pepper

1 Remove the stalks from the parsley and chop
them finely.
2 Melt the butter in a large saucepan. Add the
parsley stalks, potato, onion and celery. Cover
and cook over a low heat for 10 minutes,
stirring occasionally.
3 Add the stock and bring to the boil. Cover
and simmer for 10 minutes.

Fusilli with Roasted Pepper and Olive Sauce

Cost: £4.17
Serves 4

*The olives are fairly salty so you won't need
much extra salt. Serve with Fennel and
Tomato Salad (£1.51, page 123).*

3 mixed red and yellow peppers
8 tbsp olive oil
2 garlic cloves, finely chopped
2 small courgettes, quartered
lengthways and cut into
thin segments
75 g (3 oz) oil-cured black olives,
pitted and chopped
6 tbsp finely chopped parsley
1 tsp dried thyme or oregano
½ tsp freshly ground black pepper
salt to taste
350 g (12 oz) fusilli, rigatoni
or penne
4 tbsp toasted breadcrumbs
torn basil leaves, to garnish
freshly grated Parmesan cheese

1 Roast the peppers in a preheated oven at
220°C/425°F/Gas 7 for 20-25 minutes until the
skins blacken and blister. Remove the skins and
seeds, and slice the flesh into 1 cm (½ in) dice.
2 Heat the oil in a large pan. Gently fry the
garlic and courgettes until the garlic is just
beginning to colour. Add the peppers, olives,
parsley, thyme, black pepper and salt to taste.
Stir until heated through.

3 Cook the pasta in plenty of boiling salted water until tender but still with some bite. Drain and toss with the sauce and breadcrumbs. Garnish with basil. Serve at once with Parmesan cheese.

Apple and Coriander Crème Brûlée

Cost 96p
Serves 4

Ground coriander has a subtle warm flavour, quite different from the leaves or whole seeds.

450 g (1 lb) cooking apples
2-3 thin strips orange peel
1 tsp ground coriander
6 tbsp water
juice of ½ small orange
150 ml (¼ pt) whipping cream, whipped
100 g (4 oz) light muscovado sugar

1 Peel, core and slice the apples. Put in a saucepan with the orange peel, coriander and water. Cover and cook over a low heat for 15 minutes until soft.

2 Push the mixture through a sieve and stir in the orange juice. You should have about 300 ml (½ pt) of purée.

3 Divide the mixture between 4 ramekins and leave to cool. Top with a layer of whipped cream. Chill for several hours.

4 When ready to serve, sprinkle a thick layer of sugar over the cream. Place under a preheated, very hot grill for 2-3 minutes until the sugar melts and caramelizes. Serve at once.

NUTRITIONAL INFORMATION

First course per portion: calories 175 ● protein 4g ● fat 10g ● carbohydrate 16g ● fibre 4g ● source of: calcium, iron, folic acid, vitamin C, beta-carotene

Main course per portion: calories 600 ● protein 14g ● fat 28g ● carbohydrate 77g ● fibre 6g ● source of: fibre, vitamin C

Dessert per portion: calories 275 ● protein 1g ● fat 15g ● carbohydrate 36g ● fibre 1g ● source of: vitamin C

1 Combine the dressing ingredients and whisk until smooth.

2 Peel the beetroot and celeriac and grate coarsely, putting them in separate bowls. Sprinkle the celeriac with a little lemon juice to prevent browning. Add 5 tbsp of the dressing to each bowl and mix well.

3 Chop the spinach into thin ribbons and divide between 4 serving plates. Top with a small mound of first the beetroot and then the celeriac. Scatter the nuts over the top and drizzle with the remaining dressing. Garnish with spring onion shreds and serve at once.

Two-Pea Pie with Fried Sage and Roasted Mushrooms

Cost: £3.05
Serves 4

Don't be put off by the length of this recipe. The pie is very easy to make and most of the work can be done in advance. The fried sage adds a pleasing touch of crispiness, but leave it out if you don't have any, or use parsley sprigs instead.

Put the mushrooms in the oven on a shelf below the peas, and roast them at a higher temperature than specified in the recipe on page 122. Cover with foil if they start to get dry.

250 g (9 oz) yellow split peas, soaked overnight
900 ml (1½ pt) water
½ tsp turmeric
bunch of spring onions
4 tbsp olive oil
2 garlic cloves, finely chopped
10 black peppercorns, crushed
3 cloves, crushed
1/2 tsp coriander seeds, crushed
pinch of dried chilli flakes
salt
2 tbsp lemon juice
350 g (12 oz) frozen peas
50 g (2 oz) butter
freshly ground black pepper
75 g (3 oz) breadcrumbs
Roasted Mushrooms (page 122), to serve
small handful of sage leaves, shredded

Celeriac and Beetroot Salad with Orange and Thyme Dressing

Cost: £2.17
Serves 4

Beetroot is much nicer used raw in a salad so don't buy it pre-cooked. If you can't find celeriac, use kohlrabi, parsnip or even swede instead, and if you don't have access to free fresh thyme use half the quantity of dried thyme. Serve with warm rye bread to mop up the dressing.

ORANGE AND THYME DRESSING
4 tbsp orange juice
½ tsp Dijon mustard
1 garlic clove, crushed
2 tsp chopped fresh thyme
(or 1 tsp dried)
¼ tsp salt
freshly ground black pepper
150 ml (¼ pt) olive oil

3 small uncooked beetroot
½ celeriac, about 350 g (12 oz)
lemon juice
100 g (4 oz) spinach, stalks removed
25 g (1 oz) walnuts or peanuts,
roughly chopped
a few spring onion tops, chopped into
matchstick shreds

1 Drain the split peas and put in a saucepan with the water and turmeric. Bring to the boil, then simmer for 40-45 minutes until soft.

2 Meanwhile, cut the green part from the spring onions. Slice the green part thinly and set aside, then chop the white part. Heat 2 tbsp of the oil in a small pan and gently fry the white onion with the garlic, peppercorns, cloves, coriander and chilli flakes for 2-3 minutes. Remove from the heat.

3 Drain the peas, reserving the cooking liquid. Put in a food processor with the onion mixture, 1 tsp of salt and the lemon juice. Process until smooth, adding some of the reserved liquid to make a moist but not sloppy purée.

4 Plunge the green peas into a large pan of boiling water. Bring back to the boil, then boil for 2-3 minutes until just tender. Drain, reserving some of the cooking liquid, and purée with 25 g (1 oz) of the butter, the spring onion tops, and salt and pepper to taste. Add some of the cooking liquid if necessary.

5 Lightly grease a 1.1 L (2 pt) baking dish. Spread half the split pea purée in the bottom, pressing flat with the back of a spoon. Cover with the green pea purée, then a final layer of split pea purée. Sprinkle the breadcrumbs evenly over the surface.

6 Bake in a preheated oven at 220°C/425°F/Gas 7 for 30 minutes until the top is golden and crispy. (Put the mushrooms in the oven at the same time.)

7 Just before serving, heat the remaining olive oil and butter in a small pan. When foaming, throw in the sage leaves and fry over a medium heat for a few seconds until crisp. Pour the mixture over the breadcrumbs and serve at once.

Citrus Puddings

Cost: £1.41
Serves 4

These technicolour puddings have a very light suet crust filled with fruit and buttery juices. Make ahead of time, leaving them to stand in the roasting tin of hot water while you cook the main course. Return to the oven to heat through.

225 g (8 oz) self-raising flour
100 g (4 oz) shredded vegetable suet
about 150 ml (¼ pt) water
75 g (3 oz) butter, cut into chunks
4-5 tbsp sugar
1 lemon, unpeeled and cut into small chunks
1 red-fleshed grapefruit, peeled, pith removed and cut into small chunks
2 tangerines or small oranges, peeled, pith removed and cut into small chunks

1 Mix the flour and suet in a bowl with a fork, then add enough water to make a soft, pliable dough. Divide into 4 equal portions and roll each into a ball.

2 On a floured surface, roll each ball into an 18 cm (7 in) circle. Cut away one-third of each circle in a wedge shape, and set aside. Use the larger pieces to line 4 greased 425 ml (¾ pt) pudding bowls, pushing the cut edges together to seal. The pastry should come only three-quarters of the way up the bowl. Put half the butter and sugar in the bottom of each bowl. Add the fruit and the rest of the butter and sugar.

3 Roll the remaining pastry into balls, then into circles to form lids. Place over the filling and pinch the edges to seal.

4 Cover each bowl with a circle of greased foil and tie with string. Stand in a roasting tin of hot water and bake in a preheated oven at 180°C/350°F/Gas 4 for 1 hour.

5 Run a knife round the edge and turn out into shallow serving bowls. Break the crust so that the buttery juices run out and the fruit is exposed.

NUTRITIONAL INFORMATION

First course per portion: calories 410 ● protein 4g ● fat 41g ● carbohydrate 7g ● fibre 5g ● source of: iron, folate, vitamins A, C, E

Main course per portion: calories 555 ● protein 22g ● fat 27g ● carbohydrate 60g ● fibre 9g ● source of: iron, zinc, vitamins A, B1, B2, B6, C, E, folate

Dessert per portion: calories 625 ● protein 6g ● fat 38g ● carbohydrate 69g ● fibre 3g ● source of: calcium, iron, iodine, vitamins A, E, B1, B6

FEBRUARY

February marks the depths of winter. The dark days go on and on, and the shops often have little to offer in the way of exciting fruit and vegetables. It's a time to close the curtains, pour a glass of wine and cheer yourself up with delicious comfort food made with down-to-earth ingredients.

The flavour of root vegetables is often sharpened by frost, so make the most of them at this time of year. Coarsely grated and combined with apples or pears and a sprinkling of nuts, they make substantial healthful salads.

Raid the supermarket freezer cabinet for bargain packs of vegetables. Sweetcorn kernels and broad beans are good value and handy for adding to soups and stews. Look for cheap cuts of meat such as lamb shanks and oxtails, to make richly flavoured stews.

Dried pulses and fruit come into their own when fresh produce is in short supply. Lemons and limes are always available but are particularly welcome at this time of year, adding zest and lightness to heavy winter stodge, and they won't break the bank. Pineapples should be reasonably priced too.

BARGAIN FOOD IN SEASON

Vegetables
Brussels sprouts ● Cabbages ● Kale ● Leeks ● Root vegetables

Fruit
Apples ● Citrus fruit ● Dried fruit ● Pears ● Pineapples

Celeriac, Pear and Walnut Salad

Cost: £1.38
Serves 4

This is a deliciously crunchy and refreshing salad. If you don't have walnut oil, increase the olive oil accordingly.

2 ripe juicy pears
1 tbsp lemon juice
½ celeriac, about 350 g (12 oz)
radicchio leaves
25 g (1 oz) shelled walnuts, toasted
and roughly chopped
watercress sprigs, to garnish

DRESSING
2 tsp lemon juice
1 tbsp walnut oil
2 tbsp extra virgin olive oil
pinch celery salt
freshly ground black pepper

1 Core and dice the pears but do not peel them. Put in a bowl and sprinkle with lemon juice to prevent discolouration.
2 Peel the celeriac, slice very thinly, then cut into matchstick strips. Add to the pears and sprinkle with lemon juice again.

3 Whisk the dressing ingredients and stir into the salad.
4 Arrange the radicchio leaves on 4 serving plates. Pile the salad on top, sprinkle with the walnuts and garnish with watercress sprigs.

Braised Oxtail with Haricot Beans

Cost: £3.14
Serves 4

If you have time, complete the first simmering a day in advance to allow time for the fat to cool and solidify. It can then be easily removed. Serve with wedges of steamed cabbage.

3 tbsp vegetable oil
1 large oxtail, weighing about 1.1 kg
(2½ lb), cut into 5 cm (2 in) pieces
1 onion, chopped
3 tbsp flour
900 ml (1½ pt) beef stock
100 ml (4 fl oz) red wine
1 tbsp tomato purée
1 bouquet garni
salt and freshly ground
black pepper
2 carrots, chopped
350 g (12 oz) cooked haricot beans
(about 175 g [6 oz] uncooked)
chopped parsley, to garnish

1 Heat the oil in a heavy-based casserole and brown the oxtail pieces a few at a time. Remove from the pan with a slotted spoon.
2 Brown the onion in the oil remaining in the pan. Stir in the flour and cook gently for 1 minute. Stir in the stock, wine, tomato purée, bouquet garni, and season generously. Return the meat to the pan, bring to the boil, then cover and simmer for 2 hours.
3 Allow to cool then chill, if time, so that you can skim off the solidified fat.
4 Add the carrots and haricot beans, bring back to the boil and simmer for another 2 hours until the meat is really tender.
5 Skim off the remaining fat, check the seasoning, and garnish with parsley before serving.

Lime Meringue Pie

Cost: £1.39
Serves 4

*This is a real storecupboard pudding which
never fails to please. A little goes a long way.*

100 g (4 oz) ginger biscuits, broken
25 g (1 oz) butter
2 eggs, separated
250 ml (9 fl oz) condensed milk
juice and finely grated zest of
2 limes
50 g (2 oz) caster sugar

1 Put the ginger biscuits in a food processor
and whizz to a fine powder. Melt the butter and
mix thoroughly with the biscuit powder. Press
into the bottom of a lightly greased 18 cm (7 in)
flan tin.
2 Beat the egg yolks until thick, then beat in
the condensed milk, lime juice and zest. Pour
on to the base.

3 Whisk the egg whites until stiff, then whisk in
the caster sugar. Spread over the filling, making
peaks with a fork.
4 Bake in a preheated oven at 170°C/
325°F/Gas 3 for about 40 minutes, until the
meringue is pale gold.

NUTRITIONAL INFORMATION

First course per portion: calories 535
● protein 45g ● fat 29g ●
carbohydrate 22g ● fibre 7g ●
source of: calcium, iron, zinc

Main course per portion: calories 167
● protein 3g ● fat 12g ●
carbohydrate 12g ● fibre 6g ●
source of: vitamin C

Dessert per portion: calories 460 ●
protein 11g ● fat 18g ●
carbohydrate 68g ● fibre 0.4g ●
source of: calcium, vitamins A, C

for about 20 minutes, stirring frequently and vigorously, until the mixture starts to come away from the sides. Pour into a 30 x 24 cm (12 x 9 in) Swiss roll tin, pushing the mixture into the corners and levelling the surface. Leave to cool.

2 Meanwhile, heat 4 tbsp of olive oil in a large frying pan. Add the onions and wine vinegar. Cook very gently for about 40 minutes, stirring occasionally, until very soft. Season to taste and allow to cool slightly.

3 Cut the cooled polenta into diamond shapes or triangles. Transfer to a grill pan, brush with olive oil and grill for about 7 minutes until golden and crisp, turning halfway through.

4 Put 2 or 3 pieces of polenta on individual plates and top with the onion confit. Serve warm or at room temperature.

Red Onion Confit with Polenta Crostini

Cost: £1.01
Serves 4

Grilled polenta is so delicious and crispy that any leftovers will soon disappear. Add it to the rabbit casserole if you like.

POLENTA CROSTINI
175 g (6 oz) polenta
(yellow maize flour)
½ tsp salt
1 L (1¾ pt) cold water
olive oil, for brushing

4 tbsp olive oil
450 g (1 lb) red onions,
sliced lengthways
2 tbsp red wine vinegar
salt and freshly ground
black pepper

1 First make the polenta crostini. Put the polenta, salt and water in a saucepan, stirring thoroughly. Bring to the boil, stirring constantly, so that lumps do not form. Simmer

Rabbit, Leek and Mushroom Casserole

Cost: £3.61
Serves 4

It is far cheaper to buy a whole rabbit from a butcher and have it jointed. Pre-cut joints from a supermarket will be about twice the price. Serve with baked potatoes.

1.1 kg (2½ lb) rabbit, cut into
8 joints
flour, for dusting
4 tbsp vegetable oil
salt and freshly ground black
pepper
225 g (8 oz) mushrooms, sliced
2 leeks, green parts included,
sliced lengthways and chopped
1 garlic clove, finely chopped
1 tbsp finely chopped fresh
rosemary
300 ml (½ pt) stock

1 Dust the rabbit joints with flour. Heat the oil in a flameproof casserole. Brown the rabbit joints and season to taste.

2 Add the mushrooms, leeks, garlic and rosemary, and fry for a few minutes.

3 Stir in the stock, then simmer gently for 20-25 minutes until the rabbit is tender, turning the pieces over occasionally.

Grilled Pineapple

Cost: £1.78
Serves 4

The base of a ripe pineapple should smell of pineapple. If it doesn't, it has been picked too early and will never ripen.

1 ripe pineapple
brown sugar, for dusting
150 ml (¼ pint) whipping cream
1 tsp kirsch

1 Peel the pineapple and cut into thick horizontal slices. Cut the slices in half and remove the central woody core.

2 Sprinkle with sugar and place under a very hot grill until the sugar begins to caramelize.

3 Whip the cream with the kirsch and serve with the hot pineapple.

NUTRITIONAL INFORMATION

First course per portion: calories 370 ● protein 5g ● fat 20g ● carbohydrate 41g ● fibre 3g ● source of: vitamins B1, C

Main course per portion: calories 300 ● protein 24g ● fat 19g ● carbohydrate 8g ● fibre 2g ● source of: B vitamins and vitamin E

Dessert per portion: calories 200 ● protein 1g ● fat 15g ● carbohydrate 16g ● fibre 1g ● source of: beta-carotene, vitamin C

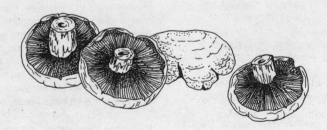

Wilted Spinach Salad

Cost: £1.97
Serves 4

Make sure the spinach is well washed. If you like, use kale, Savoy cabbage, spring greens or Swiss chard instead of spinach, or try a mixture.

350 g (12 oz) spinach or other greens,
tough stems removed
15 g (½ oz) Parmesan cheese
3 tbsp olive oil
2 garlic cloves, finely chopped
2 spring onions, green parts included,
finely chopped
pinch of dried chilli flakes
salt and freshly ground black pepper
a few black olives
100 g (4 oz) cherry tomatoes, halved

1 Stack the spinach leaves and cut crossways into ribbons.
2 Using a swivel peeler, shave the Parmesan cheese into wafers and set aside.
3 Heat the olive oil in a wok or large frying pan over a high heat. Add the garlic and spring onions, and stir-fry for 30 seconds.
4 Add the spinach and stir-fry for about 2 minutes until just wilted. Sprinkle with dried chilli flakes and season to taste with salt and pepper.

5 Divide between 4 warmed serving plates. Scatter with the Parmesan wafers, olives, and garnish with the tomatoes. Serve at once.

Florentine Bean and Tomato Casserole

Cost: £3.37
Serves 4

This is a classic bean dish from Florence. It's nice to flavour it with sage if you have some growing, but you could use marjoram, thyme or parsley, preferably flat-leafed. The cooking time for the beans will depend on their age. They should end up soft but still holding their shape.

350 g (12 oz) haricot or cannellini
beans, soaked overnight
2.3 L (4 pt) water
salt
6 tbsp olive oil
25 g (1 oz) butter
2 large garlic cloves, thinly sliced
10-12 fresh sage leaves, roughly
chopped
1 red onion, thinly sliced
450 g (1 lb) tomatoes, peeled,
deseeded and chopped,
or 400 g (14 oz) can chopped tomatoes
1 tbsp tomato purée
freshly ground black pepper
50 g (2 oz) freshly grated
Parmesan cheese
8 thin slices ciabatta bread, toasted

1 Drain the beans and put in a saucepan with the fresh water. Bring to the boil, then simmer for about 45 minutes, or until the beans are tender. Add 1 tsp salt and simmer for 10 minutes more. Drain the beans, reserving the cooking liquid.
2 Heat 4 tbsp of the oil and the butter in a large pan. Add the garlic and sage, and gently fry for 1 minute. Add the onion and fry over a medium-low heat for 5 minutes. Then add the tomatoes and the purée, and cook for another 2-3 minutes, stirring.

3 Add the drained beans, season with salt and generous grindings of black pepper. Cover and cook for about 20 minutes, adding the reserved bean water as necessary. The mixture should be fairly soupy. Stir in half the Parmesan cheese. Check the seasoning.

4 Place 2 slices of bread on each plate or in shallow soup dishes and drizzle with the remaining olive oil. Ladle the beans over the top and serve with the remaining Parmesan cheese.

Pear and Chocolate Pudding

Cost: 97p
Serves 4

Oozing with hot chocolate sauce, this easily made sponge pudding will have you coming back for seconds. If you don't have dried pears, use prunes, raisins, dried apricots or apples instead. Be sure to use a big enough dish – the pudding rises as it cooks.

100 g (4 oz) sunflower margarine
75 g (3 oz) sugar
1 egg (size 2), beaten
100 g (4 oz) self-raising flour
75 g (3 oz) dried pears, chopped
into 1 cm (½ in) pieces
knob of stem ginger, finely chopped
(optional)

CHOCOLATE SAUCE
50 g (2 oz) sugar
25 g (1 oz) unsweetened cocoa powder
350 ml (12 fl oz) hot water

1 Beat the margarine with the sugar until fluffy, then gradually beat in the egg. Fold in the flour, then the pears and ginger.

2 Spoon the mixture into a 1.5 L (2½ pt) oven-proof dish, and level the surface.

3 To make the sauce, combine the sugar with the cocoa powder. Add the hot water and stir until smooth. Pour over the top of the pudding.

4 Bake in a preheated oven at 190°C/375°F/ Gas 5 for 30-40 minutes.

NUTRITIONAL INFORMATION

First course per portion: calories 125 • protein 4g • fat 11g • carbohydrate 3g • fibre 2g • source of: calcium, iron, folate, vitamins A, C, E

Main course per portion: calories 700 • protein 30g • fat 31g • carbohydrate 80g • fibre 17g • source of: calcium, iron, zinc, selenium, vitamins A, B group, C, E

Dessert per portion: calories 455 • protein 6g • fat 24g • carbohydrate 57g • fibre 3g • source of: calcium, iron, zinc, iodine, vitamins A, B12, E

Remove the remaining peel and all the pith by cutting downward, following the contours of the fruit. Working over a bowl to catch the juice, cut down between the flesh and membrane of each segment. Ease out the flesh and set aside. Add the juice to the dressing.

3 Quarter and core the apple, then slice each piece lengthways into thin segments. Put in a small bowl and toss with a little of the dressing to prevent browning, and set aside.

4 Tear any tough stalks off the spinach, then cut crossways into ribbons. Divide between 4 serving plates.

5 Scatter the cabbage and cucumber over the spinach, then arrange the rest of the fruit and vegetables attractively on top.

6 Drizzle with the dressing and serve at once.

Fruity Salad with Lime and Coriander Dressing

Cost: £1.31
Serves 4

This simple but colourful salad depends on careful preparation. Use a very sharp knife and slice the fruit and vegetables thinly into distinct shapes.

LIME AND CORIANDER DRESSING
finely grated zest and juice of ½ lime
2 tsp chopped fresh coriander
pinch of dried chilli flakes
¼ tsp salt
freshly ground black pepper
5 tbsp olive oil

2 small oranges
1 large crisp apple
100 g (4 oz) young spinach
100 g (4 oz) shredded red cabbage
50 g (2 oz) cucumber, thinly sliced
½ red onion, thinly sliced lengthways
6 large radishes, thinly sliced

1 Put all the dressing ingredients in a screw-top jar and shake until thoroughly blended.
2 Using a very sharp knife, cut a horizontal slice from the top and bottom of the oranges.

Bean and Sweetcorn Enchiladas with Green Salsa

Cost: £4.32
Serves 4

Enchiladas are great fun to make and most of the preparation can be done in advance. Packets of ready-made tortillas are available from supermarkets and are handy to have in the freezer. You could use a chilli-flavoured tomato sauce instead of the green sauce, and the filling can be varied too.

GREEN SALSA
4 green peppers
1-2 fresh green chillies
2 garlic cloves, unpeeled
1 tsp cumin seeds, toasted
50 g (2 oz) chopped onion
25 g (1 oz) shredded spinach, green cabbage or outer leaves of lettuce
25 g (1 oz) fresh coriander
150 ml (¼ pt) vegetable stock
juice of ½ lime
¼ tsp salt
1 tortilla cut into strips
1 tbsp vegetable oil

FILLING
225 g (8 oz) frozen sweetcorn kernels, cooked briefly and drained

175 g (6 oz) cooked or drained canned
kidney beans
50 g (2 oz) finely chopped spring
onions, green parts included
2 tbsp chopped fresh coriander
salt and freshly ground black
pepper

vegetable oil, for frying
8 tortillas
75 g (3 oz) Cheddar cheese, grated
1 tbsp chopped fresh coriander
shredded lettuce and sliced tomatoes,
to serve

1 First make the salsa. Put the peppers,
chillies and garlic in a roasting tin and roast in
a preheated oven at 220°C/425°F/Gas 7 for
15-25 minutes until the pepper and chilli
skins start to blister and blacken, and the
garlic feels soft. Remove the skin and seeds
from the peppers and chillies and roughly
chop the flesh. Remove the skin from the
garlic.
2 Put all the salsa ingredients, except the oil,
in a blender and purée until smooth.
3 Heat the vegetable oil in a pan just larger
than the tortillas. When almost smoking, tip in
the purée and stir until heated through. Keep
warm over a low heat. If it gets too thick, add a
little water.
4 Next, combine all the filling ingredients in a
mixing bowl.
5 Heat about 6 mm (¼ in) oil in a small frying
pan over a medium heat. Dip each tortilla into
the oil for a few seconds. Do not allow them to
fry and become crisp. Remove with tongs, drain
briefly, then lay on a chopping board and spoon
some filling down the middle. Fold over the
sides like an envelope, then roll up and place
seam-side down in a lightly greased shallow
baking dish into which the tortillas will fit snugly
in a single layer.
6 Pour the remaining sauce over the tortillas.
Bake in a preheated oven at 180°C/350°F/Gas
4 for 20-30 minutes until thoroughly heated
through. Sprinkle with the cheese and
coriander and serve at once with the shredded
lettuce and sliced tomatoes.

Lemon and Cinnamon Cream Caramel

Cost: £1.05

Serves 4

*This is a cream caramel to beat all others –
the extra egg yolks make it really creamy.*

150 g (5 oz) sugar
850 ml (1½ pt) milk
5 cm (2 in) cinnamon stick
finely grated zest of ½ lemon
pinch of salt
2 eggs
2 egg yolks

1 Put 100 g (4 oz) of the sugar in a small
saucepan with 2 tbsp of water and heat gently.
When the sugar starts to melt, shake the pan,
then raise the heat until the sugar turns a golden
brown. Quickly pour into a 1.1 L (2 pt) basin,
turning to coat the bottom and sides evenly.
2 Put the milk, remaining sugar, cinnamon,
lemon zest and salt in a saucepan. Bring to the
boil, stirring, then simmer for 25 minutes until
reduced. Remove from the heat and leave to
cool a little.
3 Beat the eggs and the yolks and stir into the
milk. Strain into the basin and then place in a
roasting tin of hot water. Bake in a preheated
oven at 170°C/325°F/Gas 3 for 1½ hours or until
a skewer inserted in the centre comes out clean.
4 Allow to cool, then chill. To serve, run a
knife around the edge of the bowl, then invert
over a serving dish.

NUTRITIONAL INFORMATION

First course per portion: calories 185
● protein 3g ● fat 14g ● carbohydrate
13g ● fibre 3g ● source of: calcium,
iron, vitamins A, C, E, folate

Main course per portion: calories 615
● protein 21g ● fat 18g ● carbohydrate
98g ● fibre 10g ● source of: calcium,
iron, zinc, iodine, vitamins A, B
group, C, E

Dessert per portion: calories 250 ●
protein 7g ● fat 7g ● carbohydrate 43g
● fibre 0g ● source of: calcium, iron,
zinc, iodine, vitamins A, B2, B12

MARCH

Although supposedly heralding spring, March can be a bleak time for the cook. The new season's produce is often slow to appear so winter staples are still the order of the day. Winter cabbage, the old season's fat leeks and the last of the Brussels sprouts are all reasonably priced, as are root vegetables. Experiment with the more unusual varieties such as celeriac or yams.

Chicken is always a bargain at any time of year. Cheapest of all are frozen ones. You can make up for any lack of flavour by marinating and long slow cooking with spicy seasonings.

Easy-peel citrus fruits are still plentiful and cheap. Pineapples, bananas and apples are reasonable and you'll also find the first of the rhubarb.

BARGAIN FOOD IN SEASON

Vegetables
Brussels sprouts ● Cabbages, green and white ● Curly kale ● Leeks ●
Root vegetables

Fruit
Apples ● Bananas ● Citrus fruit ● Pears ● Pineapples ● Rhubarb

Smoked Mackerel Pâté

Cost: £1.45
Serves 4

250 g (9 oz) smoked mackerel fillets
2 tsp lemon juice
75 g (3 oz) quark or low-fat cottage
cheese
4 tbsp plain yogurt or fromage frais
2 tsp finely chopped fresh parsley
freshly ground black pepper
wholemeal toast, to serve

1 Flake the mackerel, discarding the skin and bones. Put in a blender with the remaining ingredients and purée until smooth.
2 Chill until ready to serve.

Grilled Poussin with Lemon and Rosemary

Cost: £3.34
Serves 4

Supermarkets often sell bargain packs of poussins which are worth snapping up. At a pinch, two birds will feed four people. Start this dish the morning before you plan to serve it. Serve with Cajun Roasted Roots (86p, page 119) and steamed leeks.

2 poussins, weighing about
450 g (1 lb) each
25 g (1 oz) butter
finely grated zest of ½ lemon
1 garlic clove, crushed
1 tsp finely chopped fresh rosemary
salt and freshly ground black pepper

1 Cut the poussins along each side of the backbone. Discard the backbone. Turn the birds breast side up, and open them out flat by pressing the breast bones firmly with the heel of your hand.
2 Mix the butter with the remaining ingredients.
3 Loosen the skin over the breast and legs with your fingers. Insert the seasoned butter under the skin, pressing it to the shape of the bird. Cover and leave in the refrigerator for at least 4 hours or overnight.
4 Insert 2 metal skewers through the drumsticks, and through the wings and breast of each bird, so that they will remain rigid when turned.
5 Place under a preheated hot grill for about 30 minutes, turning occasionally, until the juices run clear when you pierce the thickest part of the thigh with a knife.
6 Remove the skewers and cut each poussin in quarters. Transfer to a warm serving dish and pour over the pan juices.

Rhubarb, Orange and Ginger Compote

Cost: £1.22
Serves 4

Have faith in the short cooking time for this recipe, the rhubarb will finish cooking when the syrup is poured over. You'll end up with nice distinct pieces of rhubarb instead of a stringy mess.

100 g (4 oz) sugar
425 ml (¾ pt) water
juice of 1 large orange
2 tsp finely grated orange zest
1 piece of stem ginger in syrup, very
finely chopped

**600 g (1¼ lb) young rhubarb, trimmed
and cut into 2.5 cm
(1 in) diagonal pieces
whipped cream, to serve**

1 Put the sugar in a saucepan with the water,
orange juice and zest, and stem ginger. Stir the
sugar over a gentle heat until dissolved, then
raise the heat and bring to the boil.

2 Drop in the rhubarb pieces. Boil for 30
seconds exactly (the rhubarb should still be
hard), then drain into a bowl. Put the rhubarb
into a serving bowl and return the liquid to the
pan.

3 Boil for about 5 minutes until syrupy, then
pour over the rhubarb.

4 Serve warm, at room temperature or chilled,
and with the whipped cream.

NUTRITIONAL INFORMATION

First course per portion: calories 250
● protein 19g ● fat 12g ●
carbohydrate 17g ● fibre 2g ●
source of: calcium,
vitamin D

Main course per portion: calories 185
● protein 23g ● fat 10g ●
carbohydrate trace ● fibre trace ●
source of: protein,
B vitamins

Dessert per portion: calories 125 ●
protein 1g ● fat trace ●
carbohydrate 32g ● fibre 2g ●
source of: calcium,
vitamin C

Wilted Cabbage Salad with Juniper and Lemon

Cost: £2.12
Serves 4

Be careful not to overcook the cabbage, it should still be bright green.

DRESSING
1½ tsp juniper berries
finely grated zest of ½ lemon
6 tbsp thick yogurt
2 tbsp double cream
salt and freshly ground black pepper

450 g (1 lb) green cabbage
2 tbsp sunflower oil
½ green pepper, finely diced
finely grated zest of ½ lemon
sea salt and coarsely ground
black pepper
225 g (½ lb) cherry tomatoes, halved
olive oil
rye bread or pumpernickel, to serve

1 To make the dressing, put the juniper berries in a small frying pan. Dry-fry for a few seconds until the aroma rises. Crush with a pestle and mortar. Mix with the remaining dressing ingredients.

2 Quarter the cabbage and cut out the stalk. Cut the segments crossways into ribbons.

3 Heat a wok or large non-stick frying pan over a high heat. Add the oil and when it is almost smoking add the cabbage, green pepper, lemon zest, sea salt and a few grindings of black pepper. Stir-fry for 1-2 minutes until the cabbage has just wilted. Transfer to a bowl and allow to cool to room temperature.

4 Place a mound of cabbage on individual plates and spoon over the dressing. Arrange the tomatoes to one side and sprinkle them with sea salt, black pepper and a little olive oil. Serve with the rye bread or pumpernickel.

Chicken Couscous

Cost: £4.03
Serves 4

If you don't have these vegetables, use whatever you have to hand such as parsnips, turnips or swede. Cut the vegetables into biggish chunks so that they don't lose their shape during cooking.

Harissa is a fiery paste made of chillies, garlic, salt and various spices, and is sold in tubes and cans in Middle Eastern stores and large supermarkets. A little goes a long way.

600 g (1½ lb) boneless chicken,
defrosted if frozen
1½ tsp toasted cumin seeds, crushed
1½ tsp toasted coriander seeds, crushed
finely grated zest of 1 lime
salt and freshly ground
black pepper
2 tbsp vegetable oil
1 small onion, chopped
2 garlic cloves, finely chopped
200 g (7 oz) can chopped tomatoes
3 carrots, halved lengthways and
cut into chunks
1 leek, thickly sliced
2 potatoes, quartered
75 g (3 oz) chick-peas, soaked
overnight
¼ celeriac, cut in 2.5cm (1 in) chunks
850 ml (1½ pt) stock
½ -1 tsp harissa, or chilli powder

2 courgettes, cut into chunks
250 g (9 oz) couscous
chopped fresh coriander or
flat-leafed parsley,
to garnish
plain yogurt, to serve

1 Remove any skin from the chicken. Cut the flesh into large chunks. Mix ½ tsp each of cumin and coriander with the lime zest and a little salt and pepper. Toss the chicken in the mixture, rubbing it well into the flesh. Leave for at least 1 hour, or overnight in the fridge.

2 Heat the oil in a large tall saucepan over which a steamer basket or colander will fit. Fry the chicken for 4-5 minutes until no longer pink.

3 Add the onion and fry gently for another 5 minutes until the onion is soft and the chicken is beginning to brown. Add the garlic, remaining cumin and coriander, and the tomatoes. Fry for 2-3 minutes more, then add the carrots, leek, potatoes, chick-peas, celeriac, stock, harissa, and salt and pepper to taste. Bring to the boil, cover and simmer gently for 45 minutes, then add the courgettes.

4 Meanwhile, soak the couscous in warm water for 10 minutes. Drain thoroughly, then place in a muslin-lined steamer basket or colander. Place over the stew, making sure the bottom does not touch the stew. Cover, raise the heat a little and steam for another 10-15 minutes until the couscous is heated through.

5 To serve, put the couscous in a large serving dish, fluffing up the grains with a fork. Moisten with a ladleful or two of broth from the vegetables. Make a well in the centre and ladle in the stew. Garnish with coriander and serve with a bowl of plain yogurt.

Lemon and Pistachio Milk Pudding

Cost: 81p
Serves 4

This is a traditional Middle Eastern pudding. It is simple and cheap to make, and slips down a treat.

2 tbsp cornflour
50 g (2 oz) ground rice
600 ml (1 pt) milk
50 g (2 oz) sugar, or to taste
finely grated zest of 1 lemon
25 g (1 oz) shelled pistachio nuts
4 orange segments, pith and membrane
removed, to garnish

1 Combine the cornflour and ground rice in a small bowl, then mix to a smooth paste with a little of the milk.

2 Put the sugar, lemon zest and the remaining milk in a saucepan and heat until almost boiling. Gradually add the paste, stirring constantly to prevent lumps forming. Continue to stir over a low heat for 7 minutes, until thickened and smooth.

3 Chop the pistachio nuts finely and set aside 1 tbsp as a garnish. Stir the rest into the cornflour and rice paste.

4 Pour into 4 glass bowls or oval china ramekin dishes, and chill for 2-3 hours.

5 Garnish with the orange segments and remaining pistachios just before serving.

NUTRITIONAL INFORMATION

First course per portion: calories 220
● protein 4g ● fat 19g ●
carbohydrate 9g ● fibre 3g ●
source of: calcium, folate,
vitamins C, E, beta-carotene

Main course per portion: calories 530
● protein 46g ● fat 11g ●
carbohydrate 65g ● fibre 6g ●
source of: calcium, iron, zinc,
selenium, iodine, folate,
vitamins A, B6, C, E

Dessert per portion: calories 270 ●
protein 8g ● fat 6g ●
carbohydrate 48g ● fibre 3g ●
source of: calcium, zinc, iodine,
vitamins B group, C

Celeriac and Kale Soup with Garlic and Rosemary

Cost: £1.51
Serves 4

A richly flavoured and vitamin-packed soup for garlic lovers. Increase, or reduce, the number of garlic cloves according to your level of enthusiasm. Serve with warm wholemeal rolls and chilled unsalted butter.

100 g (4 oz) kale
2 tbsp sunflower oil
2 tsp finely chopped fresh rosemary
¼ tsp dried chilli flakes
1 small onion, cut into 1 cm
(½ in) squares
3-4 garlic cloves, finely chopped
pinch of salt
1 celeriac, weighing about 450 g
(1 lb), peeled and chopped
into 1 cm
(½ in) cubes
1 L (1¾ pt) vegetable stock
150 ml (¼ pt) single cream
freshly ground black pepper

1 Cut away and discard the kale stems as they are extremely tough. Cut the leaves into fine ribbons and set aside.

2 Heat the oil in a large saucepan and add the rosemary and chilli flakes. Leave for a few seconds to flavour the oil, then add the onion and gently fry for 3-4 minutes, stirring. Mash the garlic with the salt and add to the onions. Cook for 1 minute, but be careful not to let the garlic burn.

3 Add the celeriac and about 300 ml (½ pt) of the stock. Cover and simmer over a low heat for 5 minutes.

4 Add the kale and stir until wilted. Pour in the remaining stock, bring to the boil, then cover and simmer gently for about 20 minutes until kale is tender.

5 Purée about one-third of the soup in a blender, and return to the pan. Add the cream and season generously with freshly ground black pepper. Add more salt if necessary.

Black Bean, Potato and Sweetcorn Gratin

Cost: £2.86
Serves 4

Serve this tasty and colourful gratin with the new season's purple sprouting broccoli, or buttered steamed spinach or spring greens.

100 g (4 oz) black kidney beans,
soaked overnight
salt
450 g (1 lb) potatoes
50 g (2 oz) butter, melted
1 tsp toasted coriander seeds,
crushed
½ tsp toasted cumin seeds, crushed
¼ tsp dried chilli flakes
400 g (14 oz) can chopped tomatoes
75 g (3 oz) frozen sweetcorn
kernels, defrosted and drained
freshly ground black pepper
oil for greasing
150 g (5 oz) Red Leicester cheese,
grated

1 Drain the beans, cover with fresh water and boil rapidly for 15 minutes. Continue to cook

for another 15-20 minutes until tender, adding salt during the last 5 minutes of cooking time. Drain and set aside.

2 Using a mandoline or very sharp knife, cut the potatoes into wafer-thin slices. Rinse thoroughly in several changes of cold water, drain and spread out to dry on paper towel.

3 Mix the melted butter, coriander, cumin and chilli in a large bowl. Stir in the potato, mixing well. Add the beans, tomatoes and sweetcorn, and toss to mix. Season with salt and pepper.

4 Lightly grease a 23 cm (9 in) square roasting tin or ovenproof baking dish. Add the vegetable mixture, pressing it into the corners and levelling the surface.

5 Bake in a preheated oven at 230°C/450°F/ Gas 8 for 35 minutes. Sprinkle with the cheese and bake for 10-15 minutes more, until the cheese is bubbling.

Rhubarb and Ginger Tart

Cost: £1.39
Serves 4

Use the tender pink forced rhubarb with tiny yellow leaves, rather than the outdoor variety. It has a much better texture and flavour.

PASTRY
**175 g (6 oz) plain flour, sifted
pinch of salt
100 g (4 oz) sunflower margarine
1-2 tbsp cold water**

FILLING
**350 g (12 oz) trimmed rhubarb, cut into
2.5 cm (1 in) diagonal slices
2 tsp cornflour
75 g (3 oz) caster sugar
1 knob stem ginger, very finely chopped
1-2 tbsp syrup from the ginger jar
sugar, for sprinkling
whipped cream or *crème fraîche*,
to serve**

1 To make the pastry, put one-third of the flour in a bowl with the salt, margarine and water. Mix well with a fork. Stir in the remaining flour to form a dough.

2 Roll out on a lightly floured surface to a 3 mm (⅛ in) thick circle. Use to line a 20 cm (8 in) tart tin with a removable base. Chill for 30 minutes.

3 Prick the pastry base with a fork and line with foil and baking beans. Bake in a preheated oven at 200°C/400°F/Gas 6 for 20 minutes. Remove the foil and beans, and bake for 5 minutes more. Leave to cool.

4 Toss the rhubarb with the cornflour, sugar, chopped ginger and ginger syrup. Spoon the mixture into the pastry case. Bake in a preheated oven at 200°C/400F/Gas 6 for 30-40 minutes. Sprinkle with extra sugar to taste and serve with whipped cream or crème fraîche.

NUTRITIONAL INFORMATION

First course per portion: calories 165
● protein 4g ● fat 14g ●
carbohydrate 7g ● fibre 5g ●
source of: calcium, iron, folate,
vitamins A, C, E

Main course per portion: calories 465
● protein 19g ● fat 27g ●
carbohydrate 39g ● fibre 8g ●
source of: calcium, iron, iodine,
B vitamins, folate,
vitamins A, C, E

Dessert per portion: calories 530 ●
protein 5g ● fat 31g ●
carbohydrate 61g ● fibre 3g ●
source of: calcium, iron,
vitamin A

Tomato, Mint and Lentil Soup

Cost: £1.11
Serves 4-6

The first tender shoots of mint emerging in the garden are a sure sign that winter is behind us. Here they add refreshing flavour to a hearty soup.

150 g (5 oz) Puy lentils
850 ml (1½ pt) vegetable stock
2 tsp tomato purée
3-4 mint sprigs
25 g (1 oz) butter
1 small onion, finely chopped
2 celery stalks, finely diced
200 g (7 oz) can chopped tomatoes
salt and freshly ground black pepper
tiny mint sprigs, to garnish

1 Put the lentils and stock in a saucepan with the tomato purée and mint sprigs. Bring to the boil, then cover and simmer gently for 20-30 minutes until the lentils are soft.
2 Melt the butter in a heavy-based frying pan, and gently fry the onion and celery for 7-10 minutes until soft. Stir in the chopped tomatoes and simmer for another 10 minutes.

3 Tip the tomato mixture into the lentils and simmer for 10 minutes more. Season to taste with salt and pepper. Garnish each serving with a sprig of mint.

Broccoli, Celery and Broad Bean Pie with Green Peppercorn Sauce

Cost: £2.48
Serves 4

Olive oil is used to make a light crisp pastry which encloses crunchy green vegetables. Don't waste the broccoli stalks as they are delicious. Green peppercorns add a touch of smokiness to the sauce. If you don't have any, use black peppercorns instead. Serve with steamed carrot.

PASTRY
225 g (8 oz) plain flour
1 tsp salt
1 tbsp plus 1 tsp olive oil
5-6 tbsp cold water
1 egg, beaten
beaten egg, to glaze

FILLING
350 g (12 oz) broccoli
3 tender celery stalks, cut into 1 cm
(½ in) diagonal slices
150 g (5 oz) frozen broad beans,
defrosted
1 tbsp olive oil
1 small onion, finely chopped
1 tbsp fresh thyme leaves
pinch of dried chilli flakes
1 garlic clove, finely chopped
grated zest of 1 lemon
1 egg, beaten
2 tbsp freshly grated Parmesan cheese
salt and freshly ground black pepper
Green Peppercorn Sauce (page 125),
to serve

1 Sift the flour and salt into a bowl. Make a well in the centre and add the oil, water and beaten egg. Stir with a wooden spoon, gradually

drawing in the flour from around the edge. Knead briefly to form a smooth dough, then wrap in clingfilm and chill for 1 hour.

2 Cut off the broccoli florets where they meet the stalk, and trim to no more than 2.5 cm (1 in) diameter. Cut the central stalk into very thin slices. Stack them and cut in half. Thinly slice the smaller bits of stalk.

3 Drop the florets, stalks and celery into a large pan of boiling water. Bring back to the boil, then drain immediately, reserving the cooking water to use in the sauce.

4 Put the vegetables in a large bowl with the defrosted broad beans.

5 Heat the oil and gently fry the onion with the thyme and chilli flakes until just softened. Add the garlic and fry for another minute. Add to the vegetables in the bowl.

6 Stir in the lemon zest, egg and Parmesan cheese, and season with salt and freshly ground black pepper.

7 Divide the pastry in two, one piece about a third bigger than the other. Roll out on a floured surface to a 33 cm (13 in) circle and a 23 cm (9 in) circle, stretching the pastry into shape with your fingers.

8 Place the larger circle in a greased 4 cm (1½ in) deep 23 cm (9 in) diameter, loose-bottomed flan tin, allowing the pastry to hang over the edge of the tin. Brush the base with some of the beaten egg.

9 Spoon the filling into the pastry case, then place the other circle on top, so that it sits inside the rim of the tin. Moisten the edge, then roll over the edge of the overhanging pastry, pinching it attractively to seal. Brush with the rest of the beaten egg. Prick the surface with a fork.

10 Bake in a preheated oven at 200°C/400°F/Gas 6 for 25-30 minutes, until golden. Serve hot with the green peppercorn sauce.

Spiced Apricot and Ricotta Cream

Cost: £2.32
Serves 4

Milky white ricotta cheese is a really good low-fat alternative to cream. Sweetened with a little sugar, its mild flavour and creamy texture is ideal for desserts.

225 g (8 oz) dried apricots
2 cloves
5 cm (2 in) cinnamon stick
4 cardamom pods
2 tbsp sugar
250 g (9 oz) ricotta cheese
3 tbsp Greek yogurt or double cream
2 thin orange slices, to decorate

1 Put the apricots in a saucepan with the cloves, cinnamon, crushed seeds from 2 of the cardamom pods, and about 600 ml (1 pt) water. Bring to the boil, then simmer for 15-20 minutes until the apricots are soft.

2 Drain the apricots, reserving the cooking liquid. Fish out the cinnamon stick, and the cloves if you can find them.

3 Put the apricots in a blender with half the sugar. Purée until smooth, adding enough of the cooking liquid to make a moist but not sloppy purée. Tip into a bowl and leave to cool.

4 Whizz up the ricotta, yogurt or cream, and the rest of the sugar until it is thick and creamy.

5 Spoon alternate layers of apricot purée and ricotta cream into serving glasses and chill until ready to serve.

6 Decorate with orange slices and crushed seeds from the remaining cardamom pods.

NUTRITIONAL INFORMATION

First course per portion: calories 190
● protein 10g ● fat 6g ●
carbohydrate 26g ● fibre 3g ●
source of: iron, zinc,
vitamins B2, B6, E

Main course per portion: calories 520
● protein 24g ● fat 22g ●
carbohydrate 60g ● fibre 7g ●
source of: calcium, iron, zinc, iodine,
vitamins A, B group, C, E

Dessert per portion: calories 245 ●
protein 10g ● fat 9g ●
carbohydrate 34g ● fibre 4g ●
source of: calcium, iron, zinc,
vitamins A, B2, B6

APRIL

April is one of those in between times for cooks. Sparkling blue skies and cherry blossom make you feel it's almost time to dust down the barbecue, but suddenly there are wintry squalls which send you huddling indoors for hearty casseroles.

It's a good time for frugal feasters. Make the most of the last of the winter produce with some cheerful cold-weather recipes. Combine pulses and grains with root vegetables, squash, old potatoes, and the last of the winter leeks and spinach. They can all be had for a song at the moment, so don't be tempted by expensive new potatoes and early spring vegetables, although you could treat yourself to purple sprouting broccoli – it has a short season and is reasonably priced.

The new season's lamb is coming into the shops. It's delicious but pricey, so go for the less expensive cuts such as shoulder or breast. Lemons are available all the year round, but they are at their cheapest and best around now. Pineapples are also good value, as are apples, pears and the last of the winter oranges and easy-peel citrus fruit.

BARGAIN FOOD IN SEASON

Vegetables
Curly kale ● Leeks ● Purple sprouting broccoli ● Root vegetables ● Spinach ● Spring cabbage ● Squash

Fruit
Apples ● Citrus fruit ● Pears ● Pineapples ● Rhubarb

Curried Parsnip Soup

Cost: 90p
Serves 4

This is better still made with freshly ground curry spices. Try a mixture of coriander, cloves, cumin, cardamom and turmeric.

**25 g (1 oz) butter
225 g (8 oz) parsnips, chopped
1 carrot, chopped
1 potato, chopped
1 onion, chopped
1 tsp curry powder
700 ml (1¼ pt) stock
150 ml (¼ pt) single cream
salt and freshly ground black pepper
snipped chives, to garnish**

1 Melt the butter and add the parsnips, carrot, potato, onion and curry powder. Cover and sweat together for 10 minutes, without browning.

2 Add the stock and simmer for 20 minutes until soft.

3 Liquidize the mixture in a food processor or blender, return to the pan and stir in the cream. Season to taste and reheat gently. Garnish with chives.

Breast of Lamb with Green Peppercorn Stuffing

Cost: £4.69
Serves 4

It is cheaper to buy cuts for stuffing and rolling with the bone in, and then do the boning yourself, or ask the butcher to do it. Use the bone for stock. Serve this zesty lamb breast with Roasted Butternut Squash (£1.33, page 119) and minted peas.

**175 g (6 oz) fresh breadcrumbs
2 tsp green peppercorns, crushed
juice and grated zest of 1 small orange
grated zest of 1 lemon
salt
1 egg, beaten
1.4 kg (3 lb) breast of lamb, boned
3 tbsp vegetable oil**

1 Combine the breadcrumbs, green peppercorns, orange juice and zest, lemon zest and salt. Stir in the egg and mix well.

2 Spread the stuffing over the lamb. Roll up loosely, securing with string in several places to hold its shape. Weigh the joint.

3 Heat the oil in a small roasting tin, and roast the joint at 180°C/350°F/Gas 4 for 20 minutes per pound, plus 20 minutes, basting occasionally.

4 Carve in slices and serve with the defatted pan juices.

Poached Pears with Ginger

Cost: 66p
Serves 4

If you haven't got any stem ginger, use a split vanilla pod or crushed cardamom seeds.

**700 g (1½ lb) pears
squeeze of lemon juice
100 g (4 oz) sugar
1 piece of stem ginger, finely chopped**

1 Peel and core the pears and cut lengthways into thin slices. Sprinkle with lemon juice to prevent browning.
2 Put the sugar in a saucepan with the pears, ginger and enough water to just cover. Bring to the boil, then simmer gently for 10-12 minutes until the pears are just soft.
3 Remove the pears with a slotted spoon and place in a serving bowl.
4 Bubble down the juices until syrupy and pour over the pears. Serve warm or chilled.

NUTRITIONAL INFORMATION

First course per portion: calories 195
● protein 3g ● fat 13g ●
carbohydrate 17g ● fibre 4g ●
source of: vitamin B, folic acid,
vitamin C

Main course per portion: calories 585
● protein 38g ● fat 34g ●
carbohydrate 35g ● fibre 1g ●
source of: iron, zinc,
B vitamins

Dessert per portion: calories 175 ●
protein 1g ● fat trace ●
carbohydrate 46g ● fibre 4g ●
source of: vitamin C,
fibre

2 Whisk all the dressing ingredients. Pour over the vegetables and toss well. Leave to stand at room temperature for at least 1 hour to let the flavours develop.

3 Meanwhile, spread the walnuts out on a baking sheet and put in a medium oven for about 5 minutes until they smell toasty. If you like, remove the skins by rubbing the nuts in a clean tea towel.

4 Chop roughly and sprinkle over the salad just before serving.

Pork and Pepper Casserole

Cost: £4.12
Serves 4

This benefits from being made a day in advance to allow the flavours to mature. Although the recipe calls for boneless pork, buy it with the bone in as it's always cheaper. You'll need about 1.2 kg (2¾ lb) total weight. Serve with Sautéed Leeks (page 122) and, if you're catering for really hearty appetites, plainly boiled rice or potatoes.

2 tsp each green and black
peppercorns, crushed
finely grated zest of 1 lemon
700 g (1½ lb) boneless knuckle
of pork, cut into small chunks
175 g (6 oz) Puy lentils (or green
ones), soaked overnight
4 tbsp vegetable oil
1 large onion
1 green pepper, deseeded
and diced
½ red pepper, deseeded
and diced
2 garlic cloves, finely chopped
about 850 ml (1½ pt) stock
salt
2 tbsp chopped fresh dill or
parsley
8 tbsp set yogurt
chopped dill or parsley, to garnish

1 Combine the crushed peppercorns and lemon zest. Toss the mixture with the pork until evenly coated. Set aside for 15 minutes.

Root Salad with Walnuts and Citrus Dressing

Cost: £1.23
Serves 4

A very pretty salad of crunchy nuts and paper-thin circles of different coloured root vegetables. Any combination of roots would be fine, so use whatever you have to hand. You'll need a very sharp knife or a mandoline to slice them.

1 small parsnip
2 carrots
2 small kohlrabi
½ mooli (Dutch white radish)
3 large radishes
3 spring onions, green parts included,
chopped
25 g (1 oz) shelled walnuts

DRESSING
2 tsp orange juice
2 tsp lime juice
salt and freshly ground black pepper
4 tbsp extra virgin olive oil

1 Slice all the vegetables horizontally into paper-thin circles. Put in a shallow serving bowl with the spring onions.

2 Drain the lentils and put in a small saucepan with about 425 ml (¾ pt) of water. Bring to the boil, then simmer for 5 minutes until just tender. Drain, reserving the cooking water, and set aside.

3 Heat 2 tbsp of the oil in a heavy-based casserole. Add the onion and gently fry over a low heat for about 10 minutes until soft but not coloured.

4 Meanwhile, heat the remaining oil in a frying pan until almost smoking. Add the pork and stir-fry over a medium heat for about 7 minutes until browned.

5 Add the pork to the onions, together with the green and red peppers and the garlic.

6 Deglaze the meat pan with some of the stock, stirring with a wooden spoon to scrape up any crusty bits. Add to the meat and onions.

7 Stir in the cooked lentils and remaining stock, and season with salt to taste. Bring to the boil, then simmer gently, uncovered, for about 30 minutes until the meat and lentils are tender. Add more stock or some of the lentil cooking water if the mixture becomes too dry.

8 Stir in the dill or parsley and the yogurt. Simmer for another 15 minutes, then check the seasoning. Garnish with dill or parsley just before serving.

Caramelized Lemon Mousse

Cost: £1.52
Serves 4

A soft creamy mousse contrasts with tangy, chewy pieces of caramelized lemon.

**1 large lemon, plus juice
of ½ lemon
150 g (5 oz) caster sugar
1 sachet gelatine
300 ml (½ pt) semi-skimmed milk
300 ml (½ pt) Greek yogurt
3 egg yolks
2 tsp cornflour**

1 Using a very sharp knife, thinly slice the lemon, discarding the pips. Put the lemon slices in a saucepan with 75 g (3 oz) of the sugar over a low heat. When the sugar begins to melt stir

gently until the lemon slices are evenly coated. Raise the heat and cook for 7-10 minutes, stirring occasionally, until the syrup just starts to thicken and is on the point of turning golden. Immediately remove from the heat. Using tongs, place the lemon slices in a single layer on a lightly oiled plate and leave to cool.

2 Put 3 tbsp of hot water in a small bowl. Sprinkle the gelatine evenly over the surface and leave to soak for 10 minutes until spongy. Then stand the bowl in a pan of hot water over a low heat for 3 minutes until completely dissolved.

3 Put the lemon juice, milk, yogurt, remaining sugar, egg yolks and cornflour in a bowl and beat well until smooth.

4 Set the bowl over a pan of simmering water. Cook for 8-10 minutes, stirring constantly, until the mixture is thick enough to coat the back of a spoon. Allow to cool a little. Beat in the gelatine in a thin stream.

5 Arrange the lemon slices around the base and sides of a lightly oiled 1.1 L (2 pt) mould, cutting some of them in half to fit. Pour the custard into the mould and leave to cool completely. Cover and chill for at least 4 hours.

6 When ready to serve, dip the mould in hot water for a minute or two before turning out.

NUTRITIONAL INFORMATION

First course per portion: calories 175
● protein 2g ● fat 16g ●
carbohydrate 6g ● fibre 3g ●
source of: folate, vitamins A, C, E

Main course per portion: calories 440
● protein 50g ● fat 15g ●
carbohydrate 29g ● fibre 5g ●
source of: calcium, iron, zinc,
selenium, iodine, B vitamins, folate,
vitamins A, C

Dessert per portion: calories 335 ●
protein 12g ● fat 12g ●
carbohydrate 47g ● fibre 0g ●
source of: calcium, iron, zinc,
iodine, B vitamins, folate,
vitamin A

4 Reheat gently and check the seasoning. Add a few croûtons to each serving and garnish with a coriander leaf.

MENU 3
Vegetarian
Total cost £6.45

●

Carrot and Coriander Soup

●

Spiced Puy Lentils with Goat Cheese

●

Pineapple Parcels

Carrot and Coriander Soup

Cost: 76p
Serves 4

You could make the soup with mint or parsley instead of coriander. This is particularly worth doing if you have access to free herbs from a garden.

40 g (1½ oz) sunflower margarine
1 small onion, chopped
450 g (1 lb) carrots, chopped
175 g (6 oz) potatoes, chopped
3 tbsp finely chopped fresh coriander
850 ml (1½ pt) vegetable stock
salt and freshly ground black pepper
fried bread croûtons, to garnish
coriander leaves, to garnish

1 Melt the margarine in a large saucepan. Add the onion, carrots, potatoes and coriander. Cover and sweat over a low heat for 10 minutes, stirring occasionally.
2 Add the stock and season with salt and pepper. Bring to the boil, then simmer for 15 minutes.
3 Purée two-thirds of the mixture until smooth, then return to the unpuréed soup in the pan. If you like your soup without any texture, purée the whole lot.

Spiced Puy Lentils with Goat Cheese

Cost: £4.21
Serves 4

The goat cheese makes this fairly rich so serve it with a simple green salad.

225 g (8 oz) Puy lentils, soaked overnight
425 ml (¾ pt) vegetable stock
4 tbsp olive oil
25 g (1 oz) butter
1 onion, finely chopped
2.5 cm (1 in) piece fresh ginger root, chopped finely
½ tsp cumin seeds, crushed
2 garlic cloves, finely chopped
4 large tomatoes, peeled, deseeded and chopped
salt and freshly ground black pepper
4 slices goat cheese (from a log)
fresh flat-leafed parsley or coriander, to garnish

CRUMB COATING
75 g (3 oz) slightly stale breadcrumbs
2 tsp dried marjoram or thyme
¼ tsp freshly ground black pepper
flour
1 egg, beaten

1 Drain the lentils and put in a saucepan with the stock. Bring to the boil, simmer for 5 minutes, then drain again.
2 Heat 1 tbsp of the oil and the butter in a saucepan until foaming. Add the onion and gently fry for 5 minutes. Stir in the ginger, cumin seeds and half the garlic. Fry for another minute. Add the tomato and lentils, and season with salt and pepper to taste. Simmer for 3-4 minutes, set aside and keep warm.
3 Shave some of the rind off the cheese, leaving just enough to hold the slices together when they are fried.

4 To make the coating, mix together the breadcrumbs, thyme and pepper. Dip the goat cheese first in the flour, then the egg, and finally in the crumbs so that they are evenly coated.

5 Heat the remaining oil in a frying pan with the remaining garlic. Fry the cheese slices over a medium heat for about 1 minute each side until browned, turning them carefully.

6 Transfer the lentils to a warm serving dish, top with the cheese slices and garnish with parsley. Serve at once.

Pineapple Parcels

Cost: £1.48
Serves 4

If you've got any kirsch or other liqueur left over from Christmas, add a few drops to the nut paste. Or you could add a little almond or vanilla essence.

½ small pineapple
75 g (3 oz) mixed nuts, finely ground
75 g (3 oz) caster sugar
1 egg yolk
few drops of kirsch, or almond or
vanilla essence (optional)
two 45.5 x 35.5 cm (18 x 14 in) sheets
of filo pastry
sunflower or grapeseed oil, for
brushing
icing sugar, to dust
single cream or plain yogurt,
to serve

1 Peel the pineapple, remove the core and chop the flesh finely. Drain the flesh in a nylon sieve. Drink the juice or save it for another use.

2 Mix the nuts, sugar and egg yolk to a smooth paste. Stir in the pineapple flesh. Add the kirsch or almond essence if using.

3 Cut each filo sheet into 4 strips measuring 9 x 45.5 cm (3½ x 18 in). Pile them up and cover with a clean, damp tea towel to prevent them from drying out.

4 Brush some oil over one of the filo strips. Divide the pineapple mixture into 8 portions. Place a portion at the end of the strip. Fold one corner across the filling to form a triangle. Then continue folding the strip to form a triangular-shaped parcel. Repeat with the remaining strips and filling.

5 Put the parcels on a baking sheet and brush with a little more oil. Bake in a preheated oven at 220°C/425°F/Gas 7 for 20 minutes until golden brown and crisp.

6 Sprinkle with icing sugar and serve with single cream or plain yogurt.

NUTRITIONAL INFORMATION

First course per portion: calories 185
● protein 2g ● fat 11g ●
carbohydrate 21g ● fibre 4g ●
source of: vitamin A, folate

Main course per portion: calories 460
● protein 20g ● fat 21g ●
carbohydrate 51g ● fibre 7g ●
source of:calcium, iron, zinc,
selenium, folate,
vitamins A, C, E

Dessert per portion: calories 250 ●
protein 6g ● fat 13g ●
carbohydrate 30g ● fibre 2g ●
source of: folate,
vitamin E

Warm Butternut Squash and Mushroom Salad

Cost: £1.78
Serves 4

Here is a simple but filling salad of contrasting textures and temperatures: warm buttery squash and mushrooms on cool greens with a crunchy topping.

1 butternut squash weighing about 500 g (18 oz)
2 large flat cap mushrooms
5 tbsp olive oil
½ tsp each black peppercorns and coriander seeds, coarsely crushed
2 garlic cloves, thinly sliced
sea salt
½ tbsp wine vinegar
squeeze of orange juice
2 handfuls spinach, cut into ribbons
handful of fried bread croûtons
chopped fresh coriander or flat-leafed parsley, to garnish

1 Cut the squash in half crossways at the point where the rounded part meets the neck. Cut the skin off each piece. Quarter the rounded part and remove the seeds and fibres. Slice lengthways into 6 mm (¼ in) thick segments.

Cut the neck in half lengthways, then crossways into 6 mm (¼ in) slices.
2 Wipe the mushrooms, then cut into 6 mm (¼ in) slices across the total width of the mushroom.
3 Heat the oil with the peppercorns and coriander in a large frying pan over medium heat. Fry the squash in batches, turning with tongs, until lightly browned. Sprinkle with sea salt. Using a slotted spoon, remove to a colander set over a bowl.
4 Fry the mushrooms for 5 minutes, adding some of the oil drained from the squash. Add the garlic and fry for another minute. Sprinkle with salt and add to the squash.
5 Return any drained oil to the pan. Add the vinegar and a squeeze of orange juice and bubble for a few seconds.
6 Arrange the spinach on individual serving plates. Pile the vegetables on top, then pour over the pan juices. Add a few croûtons (make sure they are warm) then sprinkle with the coriander or parsley. Serve at once.

Leek and Red Onion Pizza with Rosemary

Cost: £3.12
Serves 4

A home-made pizza with an imaginative topping makes a delicious main course for relaxed entertaining. The secret of success is good flour and oil, a thin dough for the base, not too much topping and a very hot oven. Serve with a big green salad.

DOUGH
225 g (8 oz) strong plain flour
1 tsp easy-blend dried yeast
1 tsp salt
1 tbsp olive oil
125-150 ml (4 fl oz–¼ pt) tepid water

TOPPING
4 tbsp olive oil
3 red onions, thinly sliced lengthways
1½ tbsp finely chopped fresh rosemary
1 tsp green or black peppercorns, crushed

2 garlic cloves, finely chopped
1 tbsp balsamic vinegar
salt
1 quantity Quick Tomato Sauce
(page 125)
50 g (2 oz) thinly sliced leek,
including some of the green part
50 g (2 oz) mozzarella cheese,
torn into thumb-nail sized pieces
50 g (2 oz) feta cheese,
crumbled
a few oil-cured black olives,
pitted
2 tbsp freshly grated Parmesan
cheese

1 Sift the flour, yeast and salt into a bowl. Pour the oil and water into the centre, then stir vigorously, gradually drawing in the flour, to form a soft dough. Knead for at least 10 minutes until silky smooth. Place the dough in an oiled bowl, cover with clingfilm and leave to rise in a warm place for 1-2 hours, until doubled in size.

2 Meanwhile, heat the oil in a large frying pan, and fry the onions with the rosemary and crushed peppercorns over a very low heat for 40 minutes, stirring now and then. The onions should be very soft and beginning to caramelize.

3 Raise the heat and stir in the garlic, vinegar, and salt to taste. Fry for 1-2 minutes, then remove from the pan with a slotted spoon.

4 Roll out the dough to a 30 cm (12 in) circle. Place on a greased, perforated pizza pan or baking sheet, pressing it out with the palm of your hand. Pinch the edges between your finger and thumb to form a raised rim.

5 Spread a thin layer of the tomato sauce over the dough. Scatter the onions evenly over the top, followed by the leek slices (separate the rings). Sprinkle with the mozzarella and feta cheeses and the olives.

6 Bake in a preheated oven at 240°C/475°F/ Gas 9 for 15 minutes, until the leek is beginning to blacken. Sprinkle with the Parmesan cheese and serve at once.

Pan-Fried Sesame Apples

Cost: 66p
Serves 4

Use crisp English eating apples such as Cox's. They are coming to the end of their season and should be really cheap. This can be made in advance and kept warm. Serve with whipped cream if you like, but it's fine without.

600 g (1¼ lb) crisp eating apples
65 g (2½ oz) butter
1 tbsp sugar
2 tsp sesame seeds
juice of ½ orange

1 Quarter, core and peel the apples. Cut each quarter lengthways into 3 segments.

2 Heat 50 g (2 oz) of the butter in a large frying pan until foaming. Add the apples and fry until golden – shaking and tossing the pan, or turning with tongs rather than stirring. That way, the fruit will remain whole. Carefully transfer to a bowl.

3 Add the remaining butter to the pan with the sugar and sesame seeds. Stir for a few seconds, then stir in the orange juice, scraping up any sticky bits from the bottom of the pan. Return the apples to the pan and heat through.

NUTRITIONAL INFORMATION

First course per portion: calories 175
● protein 2g ● fat 14g ●
carbohydrate 11g ● fibre 3g ●
source of: iron, vitamins A, B6, C, E,
folate

Main course per portion: calories 565
● protein 16g ● fat 31g ●
carbohydrate 57g ● fibre 4g ●
source of: calcium, iron, zinc, iodine,
vitamins A, B group, C, E

Dessert per portion: calories 210 ●
protein 1g ● fat 14g ●
carbohydrate 21g ● fibre 3g ●
source of: vitamins A, C, E

MAY

May is a month of opportunities for frugal feasters. It's one of the best months for vegetables, with home-grown peas and tender broad beans making a welcome appearance after the long winter months. Make the most of cucumbers, cauliflower and spinach as there should be plenty around at this time of year. Home-grown and imported courgettes are also plentiful and a decent price.

Jersey Royal new potatoes appear this month but prices are still high. Meanwhile, old potatoes are really cheap. With a little imagination they can be turned into a tasty supper dish. Leeks are coming to an end, as are Israeli Hass avocados, so both should be at bargain prices.

The end of May is the official start to the British asparagus season. Although expensive, asparagus is not beyond reach if you serve a few plump tips with other young spring vegetables, or use it in a pasta sauce or risotto.

Fresh herbs are putting forth tender green shoots. They are easily grown in pots, so why not try growing a few varieties that the supermarkets don't sell? Lovage, savory, lemon balm and angelica will all add a certain something to the most frugal of feasts.

English spring lamb is delicious but expensive. Instead, look for frozen New Zealand lamb which can be had for as little as 99p a pound. It's delicious braised in its own juices with fat juicy cloves of the new season's garlic.

Fruit is still thin on the ground, but pineapples and rhubarb should be reasonably priced, and there are plenty of lemons and limes.

If you live in the country, the best bargain of all in late May is elderflowers. Free for the asking and hanging in creamy clusters, these scented blossoms make magical fools, fritters, custards and sorbets. Make sure you gather them away from busy roads where they are not contaminated with traffic fumes.

BARGAIN FOOD IN SEASON

Vegetables
Avocado pears (Haas) ● Broad beans ● Cauliflowers ● Courgettes ●
Cucumbers ● Leeks ● Peas ● Purple sprouting broccoli ● Spring onions

Fruit
Lemons ● Limes ● Pineapples ● Rhubarb

MENU 1
Non-vegetarian
Total cost £6.67
•
Avocado Pâté with
Crudités
•
Crunchy Yogurt Chicken
•
Elderflower Sorbet

Avocado Pâté with Crudités

Cost: £2.02
Serves 4

Don't make this more than an hour or two before you plan to serve it. If left to stand for longer it will lose its bright fresh colour.

3 ripe avocados
juice of 1 lime
1 garlic clove, crushed
3 tbsp olive oil
3 tbsp chopped fresh mixed herbs
2 tsp green peppercorns
salt
handful of crisp lettuce, torn into
bite-sized pieces
⅓ cucumber, unpeeled, cut into
fingers, to garnish
½ small cauliflower, broken into tiny
florets, to garnish

1 Peel the avocados and chop the flesh roughly. Put in a food processor with the lime juice, garlic, oil, herbs, peppercorns and salt to taste. Purée until smooth.
2 Arrange the lettuce on 4 plates, and pile the purée on top. Garnish with the cucumber and cauliflower, and serve at once.

Crunchy Yogurt Chicken

Cost: £2.83
Serves 4

The spicy marinate keeps the chicken moist and flavourful, while the breadcrumbs make a delicious crunchy topping. Start the day before you plan to serve it. Serve with plainly boiled potatoes, or Garlic Potatoes (55p, page 120) and Courgette and Carrot Ribbons (83p, page 120).

4 frozen chicken quarters, defrosted
300 ml (½ pt) plain yogurt
1 garlic clove, crushed
2 tbsp lemon juice
1 tbsp Worcester sauce
2 tsp celery salt
1 tsp paprika
½ tsp freshly ground black pepper
200 g (7 oz) dry breadcrumbs
4 tbsp extra virgin olive oil
50 g (2 oz) butter

1 Cut the chicken quarters in half and prick all over with a fork.
2 In a bowl, combine the yogurt, garlic, lemon juice, Worcester sauce, celery salt, paprika and pepper. Add the chicken and mix well. Cover and chill overnight.
3 Remove the chicken from the marinade, then roll in the breadcrumbs until well covered. Place in a single layer in a shallow baking dish.
4 Heat the olive oil and butter in a small saucepan and pour over the chicken.
5 Bake in a preheated oven at 180°C/350°F/Gas 4 for 45 minutes, basting with the buttery juices from time to time. Raise the heat to 200°C/400°F/Gas 6 and bake for another 15-20 minutes to crisp the top.

Elderflower Sorbet

Cost: 44p
Serves 4-6

Pick the elderflowers from a tree well away from the road on the day you intend to use them. Shake out any insects but don't wash the flower clusters or you'll lose the perfume. Serve with thin crisp biscuits.

20 elderflower heads
rind and juice of 2 lemons
700 ml (1¼ pt) water
225 g (8 oz) sugar
1 egg white

1 Put the elderflowers in a large bowl with a few strips of lemon peel. Bring 600 ml (1 pt) of the water to the boil and pour it over the elderflowers. Leave to steep for about 1 hour.

2 Put the remaining 150 ml (¼ pt) of water in a saucepan with the sugar. Heat gently, stirring, until the sugar has dissolved. Boil hard for 5 minutes then leave to cool.

3 Stir the lemon juice into the syrup, then add the strained elderflower water. Pour into a shallow freezerproof container and freeze.

4 When the mixture starts to harden around the edges, whisk the egg white until stiff, then beat it into the elderflower mixture until smooth. Freeze again until firm.

5 Put in the fridge to soften about 30 minutes before serving.

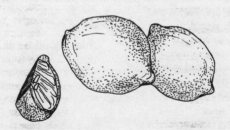

MENU 2
Non-vegetarian
Total cost £6.55

●

Tricolour Crudités

●

Casserole of Spring Lamb with Mint, Garlic and Onions

●

Apples in Jelly

Tricolour Crudités

Cost: £1.60
Serves 4

Serve with warm ciabatta bread.

½ cucumber
salt
2 small raw beetroot, peeled and
coarsely grated
2 carrots, peeled and coarsely grated
4 handfuls young spinach,
stalks removed, sliced into
thin ribbons
1 bunch radishes, trimmed

DRESSING
3 tbsp Dijon mustard
3½ tbsp red wine vinegar
1 garlic clove, crushed
salt and freshly ground
black pepper
125 ml/4 fl oz oil
2 tbsp chopped fresh chives or
spring onion tops
1 tsp finely chopped fresh rosemary

1 Peel alternate strips of skin from the cucumber. Cut in half lengthways and slice thinly. Put the slices in a colander, toss with salt and leave to drain for 1 hour.

2 To make the dressing, put the mustard, vinegar, garlic, and salt and pepper in a blender and whizz until smooth. With the motor still running, gradually pour in the oil and whizz until very thick. Stir in the chives and rosemary.

3 Put the cucumbers, beetroot, carrots and spinach in separate bowls and toss with enough dressing to coat.

4 Arrange the vegetables attractively in separate mounds in a shallow serving dish. Garnish with the radishes.

Casserole of Spring Lamb with Mint, Garlic and Onions

Cost: £4.16
Serves 4

Based on a traditional Bulgarian recipe, this simple but richly flavoured casserole is made with lots of spring onions and fat juicy cloves of the new season's garlic. If you use last year's garlic, remove any green shoots as they can be bitter. Moisten the casserole with stock made by simmering the lamb bone with a piece of onion and carrot in enough water to cover. Serve with new potatoes boiled in their skins and a green vegetable.

1.1 kg (2½ lb) leg of lamb, defrosted if
frozen
2 tbsp vegetable oil
450 g (1 lb) spring onions,
green parts included, cut
into 2.5 cm (1 in) pieces
2 heads garlic (preferably new
season's), cloves separated, peeled
and thickly sliced
2 tbsp tomato purée
½ tsp dried chilli flakes
salt and freshly ground black pepper
400 g (14 oz) can chopped tomatoes
150-300 ml (¼-½ pt) lamb stock
1 tbsp wine vinegar
4 tbsp chopped fresh mint

1 Bone the lamb and remove any excess fat. Cut the meat into 5 cm (2 in) slices, about 2 cm (¾ in) thick.

2 Heat the oil in a heavy-based casserole and brown the meat. Add the onions and garlic and gently fry until soft.

3 Add the tomato purée, chilli flakes, salt and pepper, and tomatoes.

4 Bring to the boil, then cover tightly and cook over a very low heat for 1-1¼ hours until the meat is tender. Add a little stock if the mixture becomes too dry.

5 Add the vinegar and mint, and cook uncovered for a few more minutes before serving.

Apples in Jelly
Cost: 79p
Serves 4

Use firm apples, preferably Braeburns. A few finely chopped lemon balm leaves make a nice addition.

225 g (8 oz) sugar
850 ml (1½ pt) water
2 large crisp apples
1 sachet powdered gelatine
finely grated zest of 1 lemon
chopped lemon balm (optional)

1 Make a syrup by dissolving the sugar in the water over a gentle heat.

2 Peel the apples and cut in half horizontally. Slice a bit off the top and bottom so that they stand flat, and cut out the core.

3 Simmer the apples in the hot syrup for 10 minutes, covered, turning over halfway through. Remove from the heat and leave to cool in the syrup.

4 Put 4 tbsp of boiling water in a small basin. Sprinkle the gelatine over the surface and leave to stand for 10 minutes until spongy. Place over a pan of hot water until dissolved.

5 Drain the apples, reserving the syrup, and place in individual glass bowls.

6 Measure the syrup, adding water if necessary to make up to 600 ml (1 pt).

7 Add the dissolved gelatine to the syrup, mixing thoroughly. Stir in the lemon zest and lemon balm if using. Pour over the apples and leave in the fridge to set.

NUTRITIONAL INFORMATION

First course per portion: calories 220
● protein 3g ● fat 20g ●
carbohydrate 8g ● fibre 3g ●
source of: calcium, iron, folate,
vitamins A, C, E

Main course per portion: calories 290
● protein 31g ● fat 15g ●
carbohydrate 10g ● fibre 3g ●
source of: iron, zinc, B vitamins,
vitamins A, C, E, folate

Dessert per portion: calories 260 ●
protein 3g ● fat 0g ●
carbohydrate 65g ● fibre 1g ●
source of: folate,
vitamin C

MENU 3
Vegetarian
Total cost £6.78
●
Spring Vegetable
Minestrone
●
Spinach Risotto
●
Lemon Pudding

1 Heat the oil and butter in a large saucepan. Add the onion and cook gently over a medium-low heat until pale golden. Add the carrots and cook for 2-3 minutes, then add the celery and cook for another 2 minutes. Add the potatoes and cook for 2 minutes. Next, add the asparagus, broad beans, courgette and peas, cooking each one briefly before adding the next.

2 Finally, add the tomatoes, stock, seasoning and parsley. Bring to the boil, then cover and simmer very gently for about 30 minutes until the vegetables are nearly tender. Minestrone should be quite thick, but add more water or stock if necessary.

3 Stir in the cannellini beans and simmer for 15 minutes more. Check the seasoning and sprinkle with Parmesan cheese just before serving.

Spring Vegetable Minestrone

Cost: £3.03
Serves 4

This delicious soup gives you a taste of some of the new spring vegetables. You can vary them according to whatever you have to hand. Serve with warm ciabatta bread.

**2 tbsp olive oil
25 g (1 oz) butter or sunflower
margarine
1 onion, finely chopped
1 carrot, diced
1 celery stalk, diced
100 g (4 oz) new potatoes, diced
100 g (4 oz) asparagus, chopped
100 g (4 oz) shelled young
broad beans
1 small courgette, diced
50 g (2 oz) shelled peas
200 g (7 oz) can chopped tomatoes
1 L (1¾ pt) strong vegetable stock
salt and freshly ground black
pepper
4 tbsp finely chopped fresh parsley
225 g (8 oz) cooked or drained
canned cannellini beans
3 tbsp freshly grated
Parmesan cheese**

Spinach Risotto

Cost: £3.11
Serves 4

Serve this creamy green risotto with Roasted Leeks (90p, page 122).

**1.1 kg (2½ lb) tender spinach,
stalks removed
2 tbsp vegetable oil
40 g (1½ oz) butter
1 small onion, finely chopped
225 g (8 oz) risotto rice
¼ tsp grated nutmeg
salt and freshly ground
black pepper
850 ml (1½ pt) boiling
vegetable stock, kept simmering
3 tbsp freshly grated
Parmesan cheese**

1 Plunge the spinach into plenty of boiling salted water for 1 minute. Drain, squeeze dry thoroughly and chop finely.

2 Heat the oil and 15 g (½ oz) of the butter in a large pan. Add the onion and gently fry until translucent.

3 Add the rice and stir until the grains are glossy. Stir in the spinach, nutmeg, and salt and pepper.

4 Add a ladleful of stock, and stir over a low heat until absorbed. Continue stirring and adding stock, a ladleful at a time, until the mixture is creamy but not runny, and the rice is tender but still firm to bite.

5 Stir in the Parmesan cheese and remaining butter and serve at once.

Lemon Pudding

Cost: 64p
Serves 4

50 g (2 oz) butter
finely grated zest and juice of
1 lemon
75 g (3 oz) caster sugar
2 eggs, separated
50 g (2 oz) self-raising flour
250 ml (9 fl oz) milk

1 Beat the butter with the lemon zest and sugar until fluffy. Beat in the egg yolks. Gradually stir in the flour and milk, then add the lemon juice.

2 Beat the egg whites until stiff, then fold them into the mixture.

3 Pour into a 1.5 L (2½ pt) soufflé dish or ovenproof bowl. Bake in a preheated oven at 180°C/350°F/Gas 4 for 45 minutes until golden brown.

NUTRITIONAL INFORMATION

First course per portion: calories 270
● protein 12g ● fat 15g ●
carbohydrate 23g ● fibre 8g ●
source of: fibre, calcium, iron,
B vitamins, vitamin C

Main course per portion: calories 445
● protein 15g ● fat 20g ●
carbohydrate 54g ● fibre 6g ●
source of: fibre, calcium, iron, zinc,
folate, vitamin C

Dessert per portion: calories 295 ●
protein 7g ● fat 16g ●
carbohydrate 32g ● fibre 0g ●
source of: calcium,
vitamin A

Pitta Bread Salad

Cost: £1.40
Serves 4

Serve the salad immediately so that the pitta bread remains crunchy.

2 pitta breads
5 tbsp extra virgin olive oil
finely grated zest of ½ lemon
½ cucumber, quartered lengthways,
deseeded and cut into 2 cm
(¾ in) chunks
6 spring onions, green parts
included, chopped
1 green pepper, deseeded
and chopped
6 small tomatoes, quartered
2 tbsp chopped flat-leafed parsley
2 tbsp chopped fresh mint
salt to taste
juice of ½ lemon

1 Tear the breads open and toast in a hot oven until crisp. Leave to cool then break into bite-sized pieces. Put in a salad bowl with the oil and lemon zest, tossing well to coat.
2 Add the remaining ingredients, toss again to mix and serve immediately.

Potato and Courgette Galette

Cost: £2.52
Serves 4

This is best made with old floury potatoes. Serve with Spinach Purée with Red Pepper (£1.06, page 121).

800 g (1¾ lb) potatoes,
unpeeled
1 courgette, coarsely grated
generous pinch of freshly
grated nutmeg
3 tbsp snipped chives
salt and freshly ground
black pepper
50 g (2 oz) butter, melted
3 tbsp sunflower oil
100 g (4 oz) Beaufort or
Emmenthal cheese,
grated

1 Parboil the potatoes in their skins for 10 minutes until almost cooked. Drain and leave until cool.
2 Put a baking sheet in the oven and preheat to 240°C/475°F/Gas 9.
3 Peel the potatoes and coarsely grate the flesh with a cheese grater. Mix with the courgettes, pulling apart with your fingers any clumps of potato shreds. Mix in the nutmeg, chives, and salt and pepper to taste.
4 Mix the melted butter with the oil. Heat 4 tbsp of the mixture in a large, heavy-based frying pan until very hot. Add the potato mixture, spreading it out and pressing down firmly to form a cake. Pour over the remaining oil and butter, then fry over a medium heat for 3 minutes.
5 Transfer the galette to the heated baking sheet by inverting the pan over a large plate and then inverting the plate over the baking sheet. Bake for 10 minutes.
6 Turn the galette over and sprinkle with the cheese. Bake for 2 more minutes until the cheese is bubbling. Serve in wedges.

Rhubarb and Angelica Fool

Cost: £1.92
Serves 4

Fresh angelica is not sold in shops but it is easily grown. The sweetly scented stems and leaves are the perfect partner for rhubarb. If you can't get hold of any, use 700 g (1½ lb) rhubarb instead and a little more sugar. Use young pink rhubarb – the green-stemmed stuff will be too acidic. Serve with thin crisp biscuits such as Langues du Chat or Cigarettes Russes.

**600 g (1¼ lb) trimmed rhubarb, cut into 2.5 cm (1 in) pieces
75 g (3 oz) fresh angelica stems, cut into 2.5cm (1 in) pieces
6 tbsp water
150 g (5 oz) sugar, or to taste
150 ml (¼ pt) double cream, whipped
angelica leaves, to garnish
4 small strawberries, to garnish**

1 Put the rhubarb, angelica and water in a saucepan. Cover and simmer over a medium-low heat for 10 minutes. Stir in the sugar.

2 Put the mixture in a blender and purée until smooth. Divide the mixture between 4 glass or plain white china serving bowls. Allow to cool, then chill in the fridge.

3 Stir in the cream just before serving, leaving swirls of pink and white. Garnish each serving with an angelica leaf and a strawberry sliced into a fan.

NUTRITIONAL INFORMATION

First course per portion: calories 280
● protein 6g ● fat 16g ●
carbohydrate 31g ● fibre 4g ●
source of: iron, zinc, folate,
vitamins A, C, E, thiamin

Main course per portion: calories 420
● protein 12g ● fat 27g ●
carbohydrate 35g ● fibre 3g ●
source of: calcium, iron, zinc, iodine,
B vitamins, vitamins A, C, E

Dessert per portion: calories 330 ●
protein 2g ● fat 18g ●
carbohydrate 42g ● fibre 2g ●
source of: calcium, folate,
vitamin C

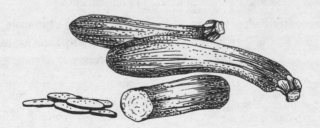

JUNE

June is the official month for strawberries, but frugal feasters will benefit by waiting a few weeks until the supermarkets start selling kilo-sized boxes at bargain prices and pick-your-own farms throw open their gates.

New potatoes should be sensibly priced, so now is the time to indulge. For the best flavour, buy them in small quantities, as you need them.

Make asparagus go further by combining it with delicious early summer vegetables such as young broad beans, mangetout and baby carrots, which should be plentiful and cheap by the end of the month. Home-produced salad material – watercress, lettuces, radishes, green cabbages, tomatoes and cucumbers – is reasonably priced too.

June is the month for salmon but it is expensive. At the other end of the scale, mackerel, herring or large fresh sardines won't break the bank and are great cooked on the barbecue. Cheap cuts of meat or chicken take on a new lease of life grilled over hot coals, especially if you marinate them in olive oil, lemon juice, garlic and spices for a few hours beforehand. Firm-fleshed vegetables, such as aubergines, courgettes and small onions, are good barbecue material, and they don't cost the earth.

Gooseberries appear in May and June. They are one of the dwindling number of fruits which cannot be bought all year round, and for that reason I find them a pleasure to use. Cooked with creamy elderflower heads, gooseberries take on a delicious flavour reminiscent of muscat grapes.

Luscious orange-fleshed melons, such as Canteloupe and Charentais, are plentiful at this time of year, but prices can vary quite wildly. Look for bargains in markets and local greengrocers.

BARGAIN FOOD IN SEASON

Vegetables
Broad beans ● Cabbages ● Courgettes ● Cucumbers ● Green beans ● Herbs ●
Peas ● Potatoes, new ● Radishes ● Salad greens ● Spring onions ● Tomatoes

Fruit
Gooseberries ● Grapes ● Melons ● Strawberries

Oriental Summer Salad

Cost: £1.85
Serves 4

This salad is full of interesting textures and flavours – peppery watercress and radishes, crunchy bean sprouts and cool cucumber slices mingled with the warm flavour of sesame seeds. Sesame oil is not absolutely essential but it adds a nice finishing touch.

½ cucumber
½ head Chinese leaves, thinly sliced
½ packet trimmed watercress
75 g (3 oz) button mushrooms, thinly sliced
75 g (3 oz) fresh bean sprouts
8 radishes, thinly sliced
1 tsp toasted sesame seeds

DRESSING
1½ tsp rice or cider vinegar
1½ tsp light soy sauce
¼ tsp sugar
salt and freshly ground black pepper
5 tbsp extra virgin olive oil
few drops dark sesame oil (optional)

1 Peel away alternate bands of skin from the cucumber, then slice thinly. Transfer to a salad bowl and mix with the remaining ingredients.

2 To make the dressing, mix the vinegar, soy sauce, sugar, and salt and pepper in a screw-top jar. Whisk in the oils and shake until thick.
3 Toss the salad with the dressing just before serving.

Grilled Marinated Mackerel with Salsa Cruda

Cost: £4.07
Serves 4

Mackerel is transformed by the barbecue. Being naturally oily, it doesn't dry out, and grilling over hot coals adds a pleasant smokiness to the rich flavour. Serve with New Potatoes with Mint and Cumin (32p, page 119).

4 mackerel, about 275 g (10 oz) each
5 tbsp olive oil
2 tbsp chopped fresh coriander
juice of 1 lemon
2 garlic cloves, finely chopped
salt and freshly ground black pepper

SALSA CRUDA
4 ripe tomatoes, peeled and finely chopped
1 small onion, finely chopped
juice of 2 lemons
4 tbsp chopped parsley or coriander
pinch of dried chilli flakes

1 Cut the heads and tails off the mackerel, then cut lengthways along the underside. Open out the fish like a book and place on a board flesh side down. Press firmly along the backbone to release it, then ease out the bone.
2 Place the fillets in a shallow bowl with the oil, coriander, lemon, garlic and seasoning. Turn to coat, then leave to marinate for at least 1 hour.
3 Combine all the salsa ingredients. Cover and chill for no more than 2 hours.
4 Remove the fish from the marinade, brushing off any bits and pieces. Place under a very hot grill, close to the heat, or better still, over a barbecue. Grill for 4-5 minutes until just cooked. Serve immediately accompanied by the salsa.

Gooseberry Yogurt Fool

Cost: £1.07
Serves 4

**450 g (1 lb) gooseberries, topped
and tailed
1 tbsp custard powder
150 ml (¼ pt) semi-skimmed milk
2 tsp sugar
150 ml (¼ pt) plain yogurt**

1 Put the prepared gooseberries in a saucepan with enough water to cover the base of the pan. Simmer over a low heat until soft. Purée in a food processor then push through a sieve.

2 Mix the custard powder to a smooth paste with a little of the milk.

3 Heat the remaining milk to just below boiling point. Remove from the heat and slowly stir into the custard powder. Stir in the sugar.

4 Return the mixture to the pan and simmer over a low heat until thickened, stirring constantly. Allow to cool.

5 Mix together the gooseberry purée, yogurt and cold custard. Add more sugar to taste, if necessary.

6 Pour into a serving bowl or individual dishes and chill before serving.

NUTRITIONAL INFORMATION

First course per portion: calories 200
● protein 4g ● fat 18g ●
carbohydrate 5g ● fibre 3g ●
source of: calcium,
vitamin C

Main course per portion: calories 805
● protein 55g ● fat 63g ●
carbohydrate 4g ● fibre 1g ●
source of: calcium, iron, B vitamins,
vitamin D

Dessert per portion: calories 250 ●
protein 5g ● fat 2g ●
carbohydrate 13g ● fibre 3g ●
source of: vitamin C

MENU 2
Non-vegetarian
Total cost £5.75

●

Pea, Sweetcorn and Courgette Soup

●

Grilled Sardines with Garlic and Fennel Breadcrumbs

●

Gooseberry and Elderflower Jellies

Pea, Sweetcorn and Courgette Soup

Cost: £1.32
Serves 4

This light, colourful soup tastes just as good made with frozen sweetcorn and peas, especially if you're short of time.

25 g (1 oz) sunflower margarine or butter
½ tsp dried chilli flakes
1 garlic clove, chopped
275 g (9 oz) green or yellow courgettes, diced
100 g (4 oz) shelled peas (or frozen petit pois)
100 g (4 oz) sweetcorn kernels
1 potato, diced
1 L (1¾ pt) chicken stock
salt and freshly ground black pepper
plain yogurt
snipped chives, to garnish

1 Melt the margarine in a large saucepan. Add the chilli flakes and garlic and heat for a few seconds to flavour the oil.
2 Add the courgettes, peas, sweetcorn and potato. Cover and cook over a medium heat for 10 minutes.

3 Add the stock and season with salt and pepper. Bring to the boil, then simmer for about 20 minutes until the vegetables are just tender.
4 Purée until smooth and return to the pan. Reheat gently and check the seasoning.
5 Add a swirl of yogurt to each serving and sprinkle with chives.

Grilled Sardines with Garlic and Fennel Breadcrumbs

Cost: £2.28
Serves 4

Fresh sardines must be the ultimate bargain healthfood. The large meaty ones are absolutely delicious barbecued or flashed under a very hot grill and served with crunchy garlic breadcrumbs and a squeeze of lemon. Fennel seeds cut the richness, but can be left out if you don't like the flavour.

All this needs to go with it is a green salad and a large bowl of buttery minted new potatoes sprinkled with sea salt flakes and freshly ground black pepper.

12 large fresh or defrosted frozen sardines, weighing about 750 g (1 lb 10 oz)
2 tbsp olive oil
25 g (1 oz) butter
½ tsp fennel seeds (optional)
100 g (4 oz) wholemeal breadcrumbs
2 garlic cloves, finely chopped
salt and freshly ground black pepper
lemon wedges
chopped parsley

1 Cut the heads off the sardines and carefully remove the guts. Rinse under running water and pat dry with paper towel.
2 Thread the sardines lengthways on to skewers. The easiest way is to pierce through the tail end and then the neck, bending the body into a curve. You should be able to thread 2 sardines on to each skewer.
3 Place on a rack under a very hot grill or over coals. Grill for 2-3 minutes each side.

4 Meanwhile, heat the olive oil and butter in a large frying pan. Add the fennel seeds, if using, and fry for a few seconds. Then add the breadcrumbs and garlic. Stir-fry over a medium-high heat for 2-3 minutes until crisp. Do not allow the garlic to burn.

5 Remove the skewers and put the sardines in a warm serving dish. Scatter with the breadcrumbs, sprinkle with parsley and serve with lemon wedges.

Gooseberry and Elderflower Jellies

Cost: £2.15
Serves 4

This will cost next to nothing if you have access to a gooseberry bush. Otherwise look for locally grown gooseberries in markets or greengrocers. There's no need to top and tail the gooseberries as they will be sieved. If you don't have any elderflowers, cook the gooseberries with a strip of lemon peel, or add a teaspoonful of orange flower water to the strained juice. Serve with crisp vanilla biscuits.

900 g (2 lb) green gooseberries
3 elderflower heads (optional)
sugar, to taste
15 g (½ oz) gelatine
150 ml (¼ pt) whipping cream

1 Put the gooseberries in a saucepan and barely cover with water. Simmer for 5-10 minutes until all the skins have burst, stirring occasionally.

2 Drain into a bowl through a jelly bag (this will take several hours) or push through a sieve if short of time.

3 Measure the liquid (you will need 700 ml/ 1¼ pt), and sweeten to taste.

4 Put 4 tbsp of the sweetened liquid into a bowl. Sprinkle the gelatine over the surface, then leave for 10 minutes until spongy. Place over a pan of hot water until fully dissolved, then add to the rest of the liquid, mixing thoroughly.

5 Strain into individual glass bowls. Chill in the fridge until set.

6 Whip the cream and pipe or spoon over each jelly before serving.

NUTRITIONAL INFORMATION

First course per portion: calories 130
• protein 5g • fat 6g •
carbohydrate 14g • fibre 3g •
source of: iodine, iron, zinc,
vitamins A, C, E, B group

Main course per portion: calories 440
• protein 26g • fat 28g •
carbohydrate 20g • fibre 2g •
source of: calcium, iron, zinc,
selenium, B vitamins,
vitamin E

Dessert per portion: calories 245 •
protein 6g • fat 16g •
carbohydrate 21g • fibre 5g •
source of: calcium, folate,
vitamins A, C, E

Roasted Aubergine Salad

Cost: £2.21
Serves 4

There is something very addictive about the smooth velvety richness of roasted aubergines. They make a tasty addition to this hearty salad.

1 small aubergine, about 225 g (8 oz)
olive oil, for brushing
1 yellow pepper
1 lettuce
2 hard-boiled eggs, quartered
8 cherry tomatoes, halved
Parmesan cheese, shaved
into wafers
salt and freshly ground
black pepper
4 tbsp extra virgin olive oil
1 tbsp balsamic vinegar

1 Cut the aubergine lengthways into 6 mm (¼ in) slices and brush lightly with oil. Arrange in a single layer in a roasting tin. Put the pepper in another small tin. Roast in a preheated oven at 200°C/400°F/Gas 4 for 15-20 minutes, turning occasionally, until the pepper begins to blacken and the aubergine is golden.

2 Cut the aubergine crossways into 2.5 cm (1 in) slices. Remove the skin and seeds from the pepper, then cut the flesh into matchstick strips.

3 Make a bed of torn lettuce leaves on a shallow serving dish. Arrange the hard-boiled eggs, tomatoes, pepper and aubergine slices on top, then scatter with a few Parmesan shavings and season to taste.

4 Drizzle with the vinegar and oil, and serve at once.

Pasta with Young Vegetable Ragout

Cost: £3.33
Serves 4

Young spring vegetables can be expensive if you don't grow them yourself. Mixing them with pasta makes a few go a long way.

225 g (8 oz) farfalle, conchiglie or
other pasta shape
75 g (3 oz) butter
4 shallots or baby onions, halved
lengthways
2 sprigs fresh marjoram or thyme
salt
3 dwarf patty pan squash, halved,
or 6 baby courgettes
225 g (8 oz) baby carrots
150 g (5 oz) thin asparagus, cut
into 5 cm (2 in) lengths
100 g (4 oz) mangetout, trimmed
275 g (10 oz) small broad beans,
shelled and outer skin removed
1 tbsp finely chopped fresh
mixed herbs
juice of ½ lemon
1 garlic clove, finely chopped
freshly ground black pepper
3 tbsp freshly grated Parmesan
cheese

1 Bring two large saucepans of salted water to the boil.

2 Cook the pasta in one of the pans until *al dente* – tender but still firm to bite. Drain and keep warm.

3 Meanwhile, melt 25g (1 oz) of the butter in a large frying pan. Add the onions, marjoram or thyme, 125 ml (4 fl oz) water and a little salt. Bring to the boil, cover and simmer for 5 minutes.

4 Plunge the remaining vegetables separately into the second pan of boiling water, in the order listed. Allow 2 minutes each for the squash and carrots, and 1 minute each for the rest. Allow the water to return to the boil before adding the next batch of vegetables.

5 Remove each batch of vegetables with a slotted spoon and add to the onions. Stir, cover and simmer. Add a little of the vegetable water if the mixture becomes dry.

6 When all the vegetables are in the pan, add the mixed herbs, lemon juice, garlic and remaining butter. Season with salt and pepper. Raise the heat and stir until slightly thickened.

7 Transfer the pasta to a heated serving dish and top with the vegetables. Sprinkle with Parmesan and serve at once.

Strawberry Mousse

Cost: £1.43
Serves 4

This is a good way of using up slightly damaged strawberries. Keep a few perfect specimens as decoration.

225 g (8 oz) strawberries
2 eggs (size 2), separated
1 egg yolk
25 g (1 oz) caster sugar
150 ml (¼ pt) whipping cream

1 Set aside a few small strawberries as a garnish. Purée the rest in a food processor, then push through a sieve to remove the pips.

2 Put the purée in a heatproof bowl with the 3 egg yolks and the sugar. Place over a pan of barely simmering water and whisk constantly, until thick enough to leave a trail. Remove from the heat and whisk until cool.

3 Whip the cream and fold into the strawberry mixture.

4 Whip the egg whites until soft peaks form, then gently fold into the strawberry mixture.

5 Pour into a serving bowl or individual dishes, garnish with the reserved strawberries and chill until ready to serve.

NUTRITIONAL INFORMATION

First course per portion: calories 250
● protein 8g ● fat 22g ●
carbohydrate 6g ● fibre 3g ●
source of: vitamin C

Main course per portion: calories 480
● protein 20g ● fat 20g ●
carbohydrate 59g ● fibre 10g ●
source of: dietary fibre, calcium,
iron, vitamin C,
beta-carotene

Dessert per portion: calories 250 ●
protein 7g ● fat 20g ●
carbohydrate 11g ● fibre 0.6g ●
source of: vitamins C, B group

Salade Paysanne

Cost: £2.04
Serves 4

This gutsy rustic salad is ideal for using up all those leftovers lurking in the fridge – cooked beans, potatoes, hard-boiled eggs. Fresh herbs and a good dressing will transform it to dinner party status. Give yourself a summertime treat and add a few asparagus spears if the budget permits.

1 crisp lettuce, shredded
350 g (12 oz) cooked new potatoes, cut into chunks
4 tomatoes, cut into segments
175 g (6 oz) cooked green beans, chopped
½ red onion, thinly sliced
3 hard-boiled eggs, quartered
4 cooked asparagus spears (optional), chopped into 2.5 cm (1 in) pieces
pitted black olives, to garnish
chopped fresh herbs, such as chives, marjoram or parsley

MUSTARD VINAIGRETTE
1½ tbsp Dijon mustard
1½ tbsp wine vinegar
salt and freshly ground black pepper
4 tbsp extra virgin olive oil

1 Spread the lettuce over a shallow serving dish or on individual plates. Arrange the potatoes, tomatoes and beans on top. Scatter over the onion slices, then top with the eggs and asparagus, if using.
2 To make the dressing, whisk the mustard, vinegar and seasonings until well blended. Gradually pour in the oil, whisking continuously until thick and smooth.
3 Spoon the dressing over the salad, then garnish with olives and chopped herbs.

Grilled Vegetable and Mozzarella Tart

Cost: £2.44
Serves 4-6

If you find the idea of making pastry a bit daunting, this all-in-one method couldn't be easier, and it's much cheaper than buying ready-made pastry. Cook the pastry case ahead of time and fill it at the last minute. Grilling the vegetables gives the tart a lovely smoky flavour. This can be done in the oven or, better still, over hot coals.

PASTRY
200 g (7 oz) plain flour, sifted
pinch of salt
125 g (4½ oz) sunflower margarine
1-2 tbsp cold water

FILLING
4 baby onions, peeled and halved lengthways
1 courgette, cut into 1 cm (½ in) slices
3 large garlic cloves, unpeeled
½ aubergine, about 175 g (6 oz)
1 red pepper
olive oil

200 g (7 oz) can chopped
tomatoes
2 tbsp chopped fresh herbs,
such as basil, marjoram or
flat-leafed parsley
1 tsp red wine vinegar
salt and freshly ground black pepper
75 g (3 oz) mozzarella cheese,
thinly sliced

1 To make the pastry, put one-third of the flour in a bowl with the salt, margarine and water. Mix well with a fork. Mix in the remaining flour and knead lightly to form a smooth dough. Wrap in clingfilm and chill for 30 minutes. Roll out thinly and use to line a 25 cm (9 in) loose-bottomed flan tin.

2 Line the pastry case with foil and fill with dried beans to weight it down. Place on a baking sheet and bake in a preheated oven at 200°C/400°F/Gas 6 for 15 minutes. Remove the beans and foil and bake for 10 more minutes. Remove from the oven and leave until cool.

3 Thread the courgette, onions and garlic onto skewers. Slice the aubergine into 6 mm (¼ in) rounds. Halve the pepper and remove the seeds. Brush all the vegetables with oil. Place on a rack under a very hot grill or over hot coals, with the pepper cut side down. Grill for 10-15 minutes until blackened, turning the aubergine slices and skewered vegetables occasionally.

4 Remove the skin from the pepper and cut the flesh into bite-sized squares. Cut the aubergine slices in half. Peel the garlic and slice the flesh into thin slivers.

5 Put all the vegetables in a bowl. Add the herbs, vinegar, and salt and pepper to taste. Toss gently to mix.

6 Spread the chopped tomatoes over the base of the cooked pastry shell and arrange the vegetables on top. Season with salt and pepper. Scatter over slices of mozzarella cheese and drizzle with olive oil.

7 Place under a preheated grill until the cheese has melted and the tart is heated through.

Melon and Grapes with Ginger Syrup

Cost: £2.30
Serves 4

Look for a really ripe melon – there should be plenty around at this time of year, and if they're slightly over ripe they'll be sold at bargain prices. This needs to be served well chilled.

150 g (5 oz) sugar
450 ml (16 fl oz) water
2 thin slices fresh ginger root
1 large orange-fleshed melon, such
as Canteloupe or Charentais
225 g (8 oz) black grapes, halved
and deseeded
mint leaves, to decorate

1 Put the sugar, water and ginger in a small saucepan. Stir over a gentle heat until the sugar has dissolved. Bring to the boil then simmer for 10 minutes. Allow to cool, then fish out the ginger slices.

2 Cut the melon into balls using a baller – otherwise cut into wedges and then into small segments. Divide among individual serving bowls and add the grapes.

3 Pour over the cooled syrup and chill for at least 1 hour.

4 Decorate with mint leaves before serving.

NUTRITIONAL INFORMATION

First course per portion: calories 290 •
protein 11g • fat 18g •
carbohydrate 23g • fibre 4g •
source of: iron, zinc, iodine, B vitamins,
vitamins A, C, E

Main course per portion: calories 525 •
protein 11g • fat 34g •
carbohydrate 46g • fibre 4g •
source of: calcium, iron, B vitamins,
vitamins A, C, E

Dessert per portion: calories 230 •
protein 1g • fat 0g • carbohydrate 60g
• fibre 1g • source of: vitamin C

Celery, Apple and Brazil Nut Salad, p.12

Oven-Baked Tomatoes with Coriander Cream, p.115

Casserole of Spring Lamb with Mint, Garlic and Onions, p.50

Spicy Autumn Casserole with Pumpkin and Sweet Potato, p.97

Left: *Plum Compote with Honey and Ginger,* p.98

Caramel Clementines with Dates and Pistachio Nuts, p.106

Pork and Pepper Casserole, p.41

Root Salad with Walnuts and Citrus Dressing, p.41

JULY

July is the month for salad, salmon and soft fruits. Even if the budget is tight there's no need to go without these summertime treats. It's a great time for frugal feasters, with a wealth of Mediterranean and home-grown vegetables, salad greens, fresh herbs and strawberries in full glut.

If the budget will run to it, treat yourself to a taste of asparagus, but buy only a very few spears and make them go further by serving with other vegetables.

At this time of year the supermarkets sell a good variety of interesting salad greens and herbs at realistic prices. Better still, try growing your own, even if you've only got a window box. Mediterranean vegetables such as aubergines, courgettes and peppers should also be cheap, as is English sweetcorn.

July is the month for raspberries, redcurrants and blueberries too, but they are always expensive. Wait a few more weeks for better prices and then, if funds allow, buy a small punnet to add sparkle to fruit salads made with cheaper fruit.

July is also a good time for fish, so enjoy it while you can. Oily fish, such as sardines, grey mullet and mackerel, make excellent barbecue material and are a cheaper and healthier option than red meat.

Although it's sensible to plan your menu, if you see a bargain, snap it up. Whole salmon can occasionally be bought for as little as £1.99 a pound, whereas individual salmon steaks cost about £5 a pound. You can cut a whole fish into steaks yourself and freeze them ready for when the weather's good enough for a barbecue.

BARGAIN FOOD IN SEASON

Vegetables

Aubergines ● Broad beans ● Courgettes ● Cucumbers ● Herbs ●
Peas ● Peppers ● Potatoes, new ● Radishes ● Salad greens ●
Spring onions ● Sweetcorn ● Tomatoes

Fruit

Gooseberries ● Melons ● Rhubarb ● Strawberries

MENU 1
Non-vegetarian
Total cost £6.98

●

Gazpacho (Spanish Iced Tomato Soup)

●

Barbecued Salmon Steaks

●

Strawberry Cornets

Gazpacho (Spanish Iced Tomato Soup)

Cost: £1.67
Serves 4

Peel the tomatoes by covering them with boiling water for 10 seconds, then drain. The skins should then slip off easily.

Serve the chopped vegetables in small bowls. If you have any stale bread, make some crunchy garlic croûtons to serve as well. Gazpacho should be served really cold – add an ice cube if necessary.

½ cucumber, peeled and chopped
350 g (12 oz) tomatoes,
peeled, deseeded and
chopped
1 large green pepper, deseeded
and chopped
1 onion, chopped
1 garlic clove, crushed
400 ml (14 fl oz) tomato juice
juice of 1 lime

3 tbsp olive oil
salt and freshly ground black
pepper
dash of cayenne pepper

1 Set aside one quarter of the cucumber, tomatoes, pepper and onion. Put the rest of the vegetables in a food processor with the garlic, tomato juice, lime juice, olive oil and seasoning. Purée until smooth. Pour into a bowl then chill thoroughly.
2 Finely chop the remaining chopped vegetables and serve in small bowls with the chilled soup.

Barbecued Salmon Steaks

Cost: £4.24
Serves 4

This is a real treat, affordable only if you find a whole salmon sold cheaply, or are lucky enough to have friends who fish. Serve with Watercress Sauce (50p, page 124) and Green Rice Salad (81p, page 123).

4 salmon steaks, about 150 g
(5 oz) each
3 tbsp lemon juice
2 tbsp olive oil
salt and freshly ground black
pepper
lemon wedges and watercress
sprigs,
to garnish

1 Put the salmon steaks in a shallow dish. Sprinkle with the lemon juice, olive oil and seasoning, turning to coat. Leave to marinate in the fridge for 2 hours, turning once. Allow to come to room temperature before grilling.
2 Place on a rack over hot coals and grill for 5-6 minutes each side, brushing occasionally with the remaining marinade.
3 Transfer to a warm serving dish and garnish with lemon wedges and watercress sprigs.

Strawberry Cornets

Cost: £1.07
Serves 4

Make the pancakes ahead of time and fill them just before serving.

2 eggs (size 3)
25 g (1 oz) plain flour
pinch of salt
125 ml (4 fl oz) milk
25 g (1 oz) sunflower margarine, melted
sunflower oil, for frying
300 ml (½ pt) whipping cream, whipped
225 g (8 oz) strawberries, sliced

1 Put the eggs, flour, salt, milk and margarine in a blender and whizz until smooth. Pour into a measuring jug and leave to stand for 30 minutes. Whisk again before using.

2 Spray or lightly brush a heavy-based, non-stick 20 cm (8 in) frying pan with oil and place over a high heat. When hot but not smoking, pour in a quarter of the batter, tilting and swirling the pan so the batter spreads to a thin circle. Cook for about 1 minute until small holes appear on the surface. Loosen the edges and carefully turn with a fish slice – or toss if you're feeling confident – and cook the other side. Make another three pancakes with the remaining batter. Allow to cool.

3 When ready to serve, fold the pancakes in half, then in half again, then open out into a cornet shape.

4 Spoon or pipe in the cream and top with the strawberries.

NUTRITIONAL INFORMATION

First course per portion: calories 130 ●
protein 2.5g ● fat 9g ●
carbohydrate 10g ● fibre 2.8g ●
source of: vitamin C

Main course per portion: calories 350 ●
protein 30g ● fat 24g ●
carbohydrate 3g ● fibre 0g ●
source of: B vitamins, iodine,
calcium, protein

Dessert per portion: calories 470 ●
protein 7g ● fat 44g ●
carbohydrate 12g ● fibre 1g ●
source of: vitamins A, C,
calcium

Drain and refresh under cold running water. Pat dry with paper towel. Chop into 2.5 cm (1 in) pieces and put in a bowl.

2 Cut the sweetcorn into 4-5 chunks and brush with oil. Roast the sweetcorn and the garlic in a very hot oven at 220°C/425°F/Gas 7, or over hot coals, for 10-15 minutes until the sweetcorn is beginning to blacken and the garlic cloves are soft.

3 Cut the sweetcorn kernels off the cob with a sharp knife and add to the beans in the bowl. Peel the garlic, chop roughly and add to the bowl as well.

4 Whisk together the olive oil, lime juice, and salt and pepper. Pour over the vegetables and toss well. Sprinkle with herbs and leave to stand at room temperature for 1 hour to allow the flavours to develop.

Green Bean, Sweetcorn and Roasted Garlic Salad

Cost: £1.06
Serves 4

This is an infinitely flexible salad. You could use thinly sliced tomato or roasted courgette instead of the sweetcorn. Garnish with lots of chopped flat-leafed parsley (it has a better flavour than the curled variety), if you grow your own or can get hold of it cheaply from a market or ethnic store. Mint or chives would be good alternatives.

350 g (12 oz) stringless green beans, trimmed
1 sweetcorn ear, husk removed
oil for brushing
4 large garlic cloves, unpeeled
4 tbsp extra virgin olive oil
2 tsp lime juice
salt and freshly ground black pepper
chopped fresh herbs, to garnish

1 Plunge the beans into plenty of boiling water and cook for 4 minutes until only just tender.

Grilled Mackerel with Coriander and Coconut Cream Sauce

Cost: £3.15
Serves 4

Mackerel's plump flesh is full of natural oils, it doesn't dry out during grilling and the skin crisps up beautifully. It's quite filling, so all this needs as an accompaniment are some new potatoes and a few salad leaves as a garnish. The sauce also makes a lovely dip to eat with tortilla chips or crisp sticks of vegetables.

CORIANDER AND COCONUT SAUCE
50 g (2 oz) bunch of fresh coriander
50 g (2 oz) creamed coconut, crumbled
6 tbsp plain yogurt
1 cm (½ in) piece fresh ginger root, finely chopped
1 garlic clove, crushed
finely grated zest and juice of 1 lime
1 tsp dried Mexican chillies
salt

4 medium-sized mackerel
olive oil
squeeze of lime juice
coarsely ground black pepper

1 To make the sauce, trim the stalks from the coriander – you should be left with about 25 g (1 oz). Roughly chop the leaves and put them in a blender with the remaining sauce ingredients. Whizz for 2 minutes until smooth.

2 Clean and gut the mackerel and remove the heads. Make 2 diagonal slashes on each side of the flesh to allow the heat to penetrate more quickly. Rub all over with olive oil, lime juice and black pepper.

3 Grill under a preheated grill on a rack positioned 10 cm (4 in) from the heat, or over hot coals, for 7-8 minutes each side.

4 Transfer to a warm dish. Smear a generous serving of sauce over each fish and serve at once. (The sauce becomes quite stiff if you keep it in the fridge, but will melt with the heat of the fish.)

Strawberry and Orange Custards

Cost: £2.22
Serves 4

You can use less-than-perfect strawberries for this recipe as most of them are puréed. You should be able to find bargain-priced punnets at this time of year.

300 ml (½ pt) semi-skimmed milk
3 thin strips orange peel
450 g (1 lb) strawberries
finely grated zest of ½ orange
1 egg
1 egg yolk
40 g (1½ oz) caster sugar
2 tbsp lemon juice
2 tsp powdered gelatine
1 tbsp icing sugar
strawberry slices, to decorate

1 Put the milk in a small saucepan with the strips of orange peel. Bring to the boil then remove from the heat. Cover and leave to infuse for 30 minutes before straining.

2 Put the strawberries and orange zest in a blender and purée until very smooth.

3 Whisk the whole egg and the yolk with the sugar. Whisk in the strained milk. Pour the mixture back into the saucepan, then simmer over a very low heat, stirring constantly. The minute the mixture starts to coat the back of a spoon, remove from the heat and leave to cool a little.

4 Put the lemon juice in a small bowl. Sprinkle the gelatine over the surface, then leave for 10 minutes until it becomes spongy. Place over a pan of hot water until the gelatine has completely dissolved. Stir into the custard, mixing thoroughly.

5 Whisk about two-thirds of the strawberry purée into the custard. Pour into 4 lightly greased 150 ml (¼ pt) ramekins: oval white china ones look very pretty. Chill for about 3 hours until set.

6 Whisk the icing sugar into the remaining strawberry purée.

7 To serve, turn out the custards on to serving plates and surround with the strawberry sauce. Decorate with strawberry slices.

NUTRITIONAL INFORMATION

First course per portion: calories 195 ●
protein 4g ● fat 15g ●
carbohydrate 12g ● fibre 3g ●
source of: iron, folate,
vitamins C, E

Main course per portion: calories 445 ●
protein 31g ● fat 34g ●
carbohydrate 4g ● fibre 0g ●
source of: iron, zinc, selenium,
iodine, B vitamins,
vitamin A

Dessert per portion: calories 160 ●
protein 8g ● fat 4g ●
carbohydrate 23g ● fibre 9g ●
source of: calcium, iodine, B vitamins,
folate, vitamin C

MENU 3
Vegetarian
Total cost £6.96

●

Avocado and Pasta Salad with Lime

●

Barbecued Mediterranean Vegetable Kebabs

●

Citrus Jelly

Avocado and Pasta Salad with Lime

Cost: £1.19
Serves 4

Choose a ripe avocado without any bruising. The flesh should just 'give' a little when you press it. If you don't have fusilli, another shape would be fine, but don't use ribbon pasta.

200 g (7 oz) fusilli (corkscrew pasta)
1 avocado
juice of 1 lime
125 ml (4 fl oz) plain yogurt
salt and freshly ground black pepper
2 spring onions, green parts included, finely chopped
2 tbsp chopped fresh parsley

1 Cook the fusilli in plenty of boiling salted water until *al dente* – tender but still with some bite. Drain thoroughly, transfer to a salad bowl and leave to cool.

2 Remove the stone from the avocado and chop the flesh. Put in a blender with the lime juice and yogurt. Purée until smooth, season to taste, then mix with the pasta.
3 Add the spring onions and parsley.

Barbecued Mediterranean Vegetable Kebabs

Cost: £3.21
Serves 4

You can vary the vegetables as long as they are firm-fleshed and evenly-sized. Serve with Tomato and Basil Salad (51p, page 123).

½ tsp dried marjoram
½ tsp dried thyme
2 tbsp lemon juice
4 tbsp olive oil
1 garlic clove, crushed
salt and freshly ground black pepper
1 sweetcorn ear, chopped into 2.5 cm (1 in) lengths
4 baby onions
16 button mushrooms
2 small red peppers, deseeded and cut into 2.5 cm (1 in) squares

1 Put the marjoram and thyme in a small pan, and dry-fry for 1-2 minutes until the aroma is released.
2 Put the herbs in a screw-top jar with the lemon juice, olive oil, garlic and seasoning, and shake well.
3 Put the prepared vegetables in a shallow dish and pour over the marinade, turning to coat. Leave to stand for 30 minutes.
4 Thread the vegetables onto 8 skewers and place on an oiled rack. Grill over hot coals for about 15 minutes, turning frequently and brushing with the marinade.

Citrus Jelly

Cost: £2.56
Serves 4

You can't beat a jelly made with fresh fruit. Oranges are a bargain at this time of year, although they are sometimes lacking in flavour. Boiling the peel with the syrup gives extra zest.

**6 large oranges
1 lime
100 g (4 oz) sugar
1½ sachets agar jelly
mint sprigs and sliced strawberries,
to garnish**

1 Thinly peel one orange and the lime, and set the peels aside. Squeeze the juice from the lime and all the oranges and strain into a measuring jug. There should be about 425 ml (¾ pt).

2 Dissolve the sugar in 4 tbsp of water over a gentle heat. Add the orange and lime peel and boil for 3-5 minutes to form a syrup.

3 Put the agar jelly in a saucepan with 425 ml (¾ pt) cold water. Bring almost to the boil, stirring constantly. Remove from the heat and stir in the fruit juice and the strained syrup.

4 Pour into a 1.1 L (2 pt) lightly oiled mould. Cover with clingfilm, and leave to set for a few hours in a cool place.

5 Run the tip of a knife around the edge of the jelly and dip the mould in hot water for a few seconds. Turn out on to a serving dish and garnish with mint sprigs and strawberries. Serve at once.

NUTRITIONAL INFORMATION

First course per portion: calories 265 ●
protein 9g ● fat 8g ●
carbohydrate 42g ● fibre 3g ●
source of: vitamins C, E,
calcium, fibre

Main course per portion: calories 170 ●
protein 4g ● fat 13g ●
carbohydrate 10g ● fibre 3g ●
source of: vitamin C, fibre, selenium,
beta-carotene

Dessert per portion: calories 165 ●
protein 2g ● fat 0g ●
carbohydrate 42g ● fibre 7g ●
source of: vitamin C, calcium,
fibre

Aubergine Bruschetta

Cost: £1.66
Serves 4

The combination of rich soft-textured aubergine on warm crusty bread is out of this world. Try different toppings using anything you have to hand, such as strips of roasted red or yellow pepper, sliced olives, tomatoes or slivers of cheese. Or simplest of all, just eat the bread with good fruity olive oil and crushed garlic.

1 small aubergine, about 225 g (8 oz)
olive oil, for brushing
8 x 1½ cm (¾ in) thick slices
ciabatta or good crusty bread
4 garlic cloves
olive oil
salt and freshly ground black pepper

1 Cut the aubergine crossways into thickish slices and brush lightly with oil. Arrange in a single layer in a roasting tin. Roast in a preheated oven at 200°C/400°F/Gas 4 for 15-20 minutes, turning occasionally, until slightly blackened.

2 Put the bread under a hot grill, or even better, over hot coals. Grill until golden on both sides.
3 Mash the garlic with the back of a knife and rub over one side of the hot bread.
4 Put the bread on a serving dish and drizzle with olive oil, and a light sprinkling of salt and pepper. Top with the aubergine slices and serve while still warm.

Pasta with Courgettes, Lemon and Rosemary

Cost: £2.73
Serves 4

Serve with Tomato and Basil Salad (51p, page 123).

450 g (1 lb) courgettes, cut into
matchstick strips
salt
8 tbsp olive oil
2 garlic cloves, finely chopped
2 tbsp finely chopped fresh
rosemary
finely grated zest of 2 lemons
freshly ground black pepper
350 g (12 oz) fettuccine, linguine
or spaghetti
50 g (2 oz) freshly grated
Parmesan cheese

1 Put the courgettes in a colander, sprinkle with salt and drain for 1 hour. Pat dry with paper towel.
2 Heat the oil and fry the courgettes with the garlic, rosemary and lemon zest, until just tender. Season to taste.
3 Cook the pasta in plenty of boiling salted water until *al dente* – tender but still firm to bite.
4 Drain the pasta and toss with half the courgettes and half the cheese. Transfer to a heated serving dish and spoon the remaining sauce over the top. Sprinkle with the remaining Parmesan cheese and serve at once.

Gingered Fruit Kebabs

Cost: £2.26
Serves 4

Vary the fruit if you like, but choose firm-fleshed varieties which won't disintegrate when heated.

100 g (4 oz) firm strawberries
2 nectarines
2 plums
1 small pineapple
2 cm (¾ in) piece fresh
ginger root
lemon juice
50 g (2 oz) butter
muscovado sugar

1 Rinse the strawberries briefly, remove the green hulls and pat dry with paper towel.
2 Cut the nectarines and plums in half vertically and ease out the stones. Cut the flesh into neat segments. Cut the pineapple into even-sized chunks. Cut the ginger into wafer-thin slices.
3 Thread the fruit and ginger slices onto 8 metal skewers. There should be 2-3 slices of ginger per skewer. If not grilling immediately, brush with lemon juice to prevent discolouration.

4 Melt the butter and brush over the fruit. Sprinkle with sugar.
5 Place under a very hot grill or over hot coals, and grill for 5-8 minutes until golden, turning occasionally and brushing with butter. Serve immediately.

NUTRITIONAL INFORMATION

First course per portion: calories 235 ●
protein 8g ● fat 5g ●
carbohydrate 43g ● fibre 2g ●
source of: calcium, iron,
selenium, folate

Main course per portion: calories 590 ●
protein 18g ● fat 29g ●
carbohydrate 69g ● fibre 4g ●
source of: calcium, iron, zinc,
B vitamins, vitamins A, C, E

Dessert per portion: calories 170 ●
protein 1g ● fat 11g ●
carbohydrate 18g ● fibre 2g ●
source of: vitamins A, C

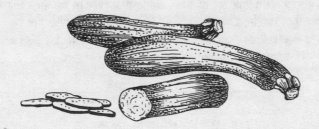

AUGUST

August is a month of opportunity for frugal feasters. Vegetables, salad greens, herbs and fruit are in abundance, with many of the summer treats in glut or coming to an end of their season.

Salads are still the number one choice for cheapness. Liven them up with unusual leaves and herbs, ideally grown yourself or begged from a neighbour. Rocket, sorrel, lamb's lettuce and mustard greens grow like weeds and it's still not too late to sow them.

The cheapest meat is still chicken, and as long as it's marinated and flavoured with zesty herbs and spices, frozen is an even better bargain. Or perhaps try rabbit for a change. The texture and flavour is not dissimilar to chicken. Rabbit meat tends to be dry, but a leisurely marinade in olive oil and lemon juice makes it an ideal candidate for the barbecue.

Raspberries, blueberries, redcurrants and blackcurrants, although not exactly cheap, should all be at more sensible prices. Used sparingly and combined with other ingredients, these delicious soft fruits can be made to go a long way. Nectarines and peaches should be really cheap by now, I have found nectarines in my local market for as little as 12p each.

August is also a good time for melons. Honeydews are by far the cheapest but they can be a bit tasteless. If you pick a good one, the flavour is excellent. Luscious red-fleshed watermelons are also a bargain and make an instant no-fuss dessert.

BARGAIN FOOD IN SEASON

Vegetables

Aubergines ● Cauliflowers ● Courgettes ● Cucumbers ● Green beans ●
Herbs ● Peppers ● Potatoes ● Salad greens ● Sweetcorn ● Tomatoes

Fruit

Melons ● Nectarines ● Peaches ● Strawberries

Marinated Barbecued Rabbit with Spicy Roasted Sweetcorn and Potatoes

Cost: £3.97
Serves 4

It is cheaper to buy a whole rabbit than portions. Ask your butcher to chop it up for you. Marinate for as long as possible, preferably overnight. Serve with Minted Yogurt and Cucumber Sauce (58p, page 124).

1 rabbit, cut into joints
oil for brushing
3 medium potatoes, unpeeled
4 tbsp vegetable oil
½ tsp paprika
large pinch of cayenne
salt and freshly ground black pepper
2 sweetcorn ears, cut into
5 cm (2 in) pieces
salad leaves and tomato slices,
to serve

MARINADE
4 tbsp olive oil
juice and finely grated zest of
½ lemon
1 garlic clove, finely chopped
2 tsp dried oregano
¼ tsp dried chilli flakes
salt and freshly ground black pepper

1 Make 1 or 2 incisions in the rabbit pieces to allow the marinade to penetrate more fully. Arrange in a single layer in a dish.
2 Combine the marinade ingredients and pour over the rabbit, turning to coat. Leave in a cool place for at least 2 hours or overnight, turning occasionally.
3 Boil the potatoes in their skins for 10 minutes. Drain and allow to cool slightly. Peel off the skins and cut each potato lengthways into 8 segments.
4 Heat the oil in a roasting tin until very hot. Add the potatoes, spreading them out in a single layer. Sprinkle with paprika, cayenne, and salt and pepper, turning so they are well-coated. Roast at 220°C/425°F/Gas 7 for 20 minutes, then add the sweetcorn. Roast for

---

MENU 1
Non-vegetarian
Total cost £6.99

●

Tuna Pâté with Melba Toast

●

Marinated Barbecued Rabbit with Spicy Roasted Sweetcorn and Potatoes

●

Two Melon Salad

Tuna Pâté with Melba Toast

Cost: £1.38
Serves 4

This quickly-made starter leaves you plenty of time to concentrate on barbecuing the main course. Serve well chilled.

175 g (6 oz) can tuna, drained
100 g (4 oz) butter, diced
juice of 1 lemon
4 tbsp whipping cream
pinch of cayenne pepper
salt and freshly ground
black pepper
4 very thin slices white bread,
crusts removed

1 Put the tuna, butter and lemon juice in a food processor and whizz until smooth. Add the cream and seasonings and whizz again. Chill until ready to serve.
2 Bake the bread in a preheated oven at 175°C/375°F/Gas 4 for 8-10 minutes until curled and crisp. Wrap in a napkin to keep it warm.

another 25 minutes, turning occasionally until the potatoes are golden and crisp, and the sweetcorn is slightly blackened. Drain on paper towel and allow to cool slightly.

5 When you've added the sweetcorn to the potatoes, place the rabbit joints on a rack over hot coals. Sear on both sides until brown. Raise the rack and grill slowly for about 25 minutes, turning occasionally and brushing with the remaining marinade. Pierce the thickest part with a skewer. The rabbit is cooked when the juices run clear.

6 Arrange the salad greens and tomato slices on a large serving dish with the rabbit, potatoes and sweetcorn on top. Spoon over some of the yogurt sauce and serve at once.

Two Melon Salad

Cost: £1.64
Serves 4

If you want to be daring, sprinkle this with a little coarsely ground black pepper, or a pinch of dried chilli flakes.

900 g (2 lb) watermelon, peeled and cut into segments
1 ripe honeydew melon, peeled and cut into segments

caster sugar
juice of ½ lemon
juice of ½ orange
mint sprigs, to garnish

1 Put the prepared melons in a bowl and sprinkle with caster sugar. Leave to stand for 1-2 hours to let the juices mingle.

2 Sprinkle with the fruit juices and garnish with mint.

NUTRITIONAL INFORMATION

First course per portion: calories 395 ●
protein 13g ● fat 30g ●
carbohydrate 12g ●
fibre less than 1g ● source of: niacin,
vitamins A, B6, B12

Main course per portion: calories 520 ●
protein 33g ● fat 30g ●
carbohydrate 31g ● fibre 3g ●
source of: iron, zinc, selenium,
vitamins A, B group, C, E

Dessert per portion: calories 75 ●
protein 1g ● fat 1g ●
carbohydrate 17g ● fibre 1g ●
source of: vitamin C

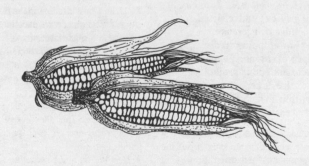

Ricotta, Walnut and Herb Dip with Crudités

Cost: £2.23
Serves 4

The herbs I have used grow like weeds in my garden, but you can use any combination, or one sort only, preferably gathered free from your own garden or a friend's. Lovage, flat-leafed parsley, thyme or mint are good alternatives. For the crudités, use whatever crisp crunchy vegetables you have to hand. You'll need about 600 g (1¼ lb) in all.

250 g (9 oz) ricotta cheese
2 tbsp plain yogurt
1 tsp sea salt
½ tsp freshly ground black pepper
1 tbsp each chopped fresh sorrel,
rocket, coriander and chives
15 g (½ oz) walnuts, chopped
raw vegetables such as green pepper,
tender celery stalks, young carrots,
cauliflower florets, radishes, cut into
chunks or strips

1 Mix together the ricotta and yogurt and season with salt and pepper. Stir in the herbs, then sprinkle with the chopped walnuts.

2 Divide the ricotta mixture between 4 small serving bowls. Place the bowls on individual plates and arrange a selection of vegetables around the edge.

Spicy Chicken Burgers with Grilled Sweetcorn

Cost: £2.93
Serves 4

Make these in advance and chill until ready to grill. Dark meat has a better flavour and texture than breast meat. Make sure the burgers are cooked all the way through and no longer pink.
Serve with skewered chunks of sweetcorn, brushed with oil and grilled until beginning to blacken slightly.

1 onion, finely chopped
2 tbsp groundnut oil
1 fresh green chilli, deseeded and finely
chopped
2.5 cm (1 in) piece fresh ginger root,
finely chopped
2 garlic cloves, finely chopped
1 tsp coriander seeds, crushed
½ tsp cumin seeds, crushed
1 tsp salt
4 tbsp plain yogurt
800 g (1¾ lb) frozen chicken quarters,
defrosted
50 g (2 oz) fresh breadcrumbs
oil for brushing
1 small lettuce
2 grilled sweetcorn ears, to serve

1 Fry the onion in the oil over a medium-low heat for 20 minutes until very soft. Add the chilli, ginger, garlic, coriander, cumin and salt. Gently fry for 3-4 minutes. Stir in 3 tbsp of the yogurt and cook for another 30 seconds, scraping up any residue from the bottom of the pan. Remove from the heat and allow to cool completely.
2 Bone the chicken and discard the skin. Finely dice the flesh, or mince in a food processor in several batches.

3 Put the chicken in a bowl with the cooled onion mixture, breadcrumbs and remaining yogurt. Mix well with a fork.

4 Form the mixture into 8 balls, rolling them in your palm to firm them. Flatten into patties about 1 cm (½ in) thick.

5 Brush the patties with oil. Place on a rack over a barbecue or under a preheated hot grill for 6-8 minutes each side until cooked through.

6 Arrange the lettuce leaves in a shallow serving dish. Place the burgers on top and scatter with chunks of grilled sweetcorn.

Nectarine Clafoutis

Cost: £1.30
Serves 4

No need to deprive yourself of luscious nectarines on grounds of expense. They should be at rock bottom prices at this time of year, and you can eke them out by cooking them in a batter. If nectarines are unavailable, use peaches instead.

BATTER
200 ml (7 fl oz) semi-skimmed milk
40 g (1½ oz) sugar
2 eggs
2 tsp vanilla extract
pinch of salt
45 g (1¾ oz) sifted flour

2 large nectarines, peeled, stoned and
sliced into segments
oil for greasing
sugar to taste
whipped cream or plain yogurt,
to serve

1 Put all the batter ingredients in a blender and whizz for about 1 minute until very smooth.

2 Lightly grease a 1.5 L (2½ pt) shallow ovenproof dish. Pour in enough batter to cover the bottom by 6 mm (¼ in). Bake for 7-10 minutes in a preheated oven at 190°C/375°F/Gas 5 until just set. Remove from the oven.

3 Spread the nectarines evenly over the cooked batter. Sprinkle with sugar to taste. Pour the rest of the batter over the nectarines.

4 Bake for about 1 hour until puffy and brown. Sprinkle with sugar. Serve hot, warm or at room temperature with the whipped cream or yogurt. The pudding will sink as it cools.

NUTRITIONAL INFORMATION

First course per portion: calories 145 ●
protein 8g ● fat 10g ●
carbohydrate 6g ● fibre 2g ●
source of: calcium, zinc,
folate, beta-carotene,
vitamins B12, C

Main course per portion: calories 370 ●
protein 34g ● fat 17g ●
carbohydrate 24g ● fibre 3g ●
source of: iron, zinc, selenium, iodine,
vitamins B, E

Dessert per portion: calories 210 ●
protein 9g ● fat 7g ●
carbohydrate 31g ● fibre 1g ●
source of: calcium, iron, zinc, iodine,
vitamins A, B, C, E

Herbed Sorrel Custards

Cost: £1.69
Serves 4

Sorrel grows like a weed but is expensive to buy in the shops. If you don't have access to a free supply, line the base of the ramekins with 2-3 blanched and dried young spinach leaves (stalks removed) and leave out the butter.

large handful of mixed fresh herbs
(eg chives, parsley, marjoram,
thyme, lovage), roughly chopped
300 ml (½ pt) milk
75 g (3 oz) trimmed sorrel leaves,
roughly chopped
15 g (½ oz) butter
1 egg
2 egg yolks
salt and freshly ground black
pepper
bunch of watercress, trimmed

1 Put the herbs in a saucepan with the milk. Bring almost to the boil, remove from the heat and leave to infuse for 30 minutes. Stir occasionally and press the herbs with a wooden spoon to release their flavour.

2 Put the sorrel in a small saucepan with the butter. Heat gently, stirring, until the sorrel turns to a purée. Spread the purée over the base of 4 lightly greased 150 ml (¼ pt) ramekins.

3 Whisk the egg and the yolks. Strain the milk and stir into the eggs. Season to taste and pour the mixture into the ramekins. Set the ramekins in a roasting tin with enough boiling water to come halfway up their sides.

4 Bake in a preheated oven at 190°C/375°F/Gas 5 for 30-35 minutes until set in the middle. Remove from the oven and leave to stand for a few minutes.

5 Divide the watercress between 4 plates, then turn out the custards on top.

Cauliflower Provençal

Cost: £3.50
Serves 4

Serve with Mushrooms and Green Beans with Coriander (£1.70, page 122).

7 tbsp olive oil
2 onions, finely chopped
3 garlic cloves, finely chopped
400 g (14 oz) can chopped
tomatoes
1 tsp dried oregano
3 tbsp chopped fresh parsley
salt and freshly ground black
pepper
100 g (4 oz) wholemeal
breadcrumbs
finely grated zest of ½ lemon
1 cauliflower, divided into florets
handful of pitted black
olives, sliced

1 Heat 4 tbsp of the olive oil in a saucepan and gently fry the onion for 5 minutes until soft. Add the garlic and fry for 1 minute. Next, stir in the tomatoes, oregano, 2 tbsp of parsley, and salt and pepper. Simmer gently for about 30 minutes until thick.

2 Meanwhile, combine the breadcrumbs with the lemon zest, remaining parsley and garlic, and salt and pepper.

3 Put the cauliflower florets in a shallow ovenproof dish. Pour over the tomato sauce and top with the breadcrumb mixture. Sprinkle with the olives.

4 Cover with foil and bake in a preheated oven at 200°C/400°F/Gas 6 for 20 minutes. Remove the foil and bake for another 15 minutes until the top is brown and crisp.

Bread and Butter Pudding with Summer Fruits

Cost: £1.68
Serves 4

This will cost next to nothing if you pick some blackberries yourself.

6 x 1 cm (½ in) slices white bread, crusts removed
50 g (2 oz) butter or sunflower margarine
100 g (4 oz) mixed berries, such as redcurrants, blackcurrants, raspberries, blackberries
50 g (2 oz) caster sugar
2 eggs
600 ml (1 pt) milk
1 tsp vanilla essence

1 Lightly butter the bread and cut into fingers. Arrange half the fingers in a lightly greased 1.1 L (2 pt) ovenproof dish. Sprinkle with the berries and half the sugar.

2 Top with the remaining bread, spread side uppermost. Sprinkle with the remaining sugar.

3 Beat together the eggs, milk and vanilla essence and pour over the bread. Leave to stand for 30 minutes to allow the bread to absorb the liquid.

4 Bake in a preheated oven at 170°C/325°F/Gas 3 for 1 hour until puffy and golden brown.

NUTRITIONAL INFORMATION

First course per portion: calories 125 ● protein 7g ● fat 9g ● carbohydrate 5g ● fibre 1g ● source of: calcium, iron, zinc, iodine, vitamins B2, B12, A

Main course per portion: calories 315 ● protein 8g ● fat 22g ● carbohydrate 22g ● fibre 6g ● source of: iron, zinc, vitamins A, C, E, folate

Dessert per portion: calories 300 ● protein 12g ● fat 17g ● carbohydrate 27g ● fibre 2g ● source of: vitamins A, C, E, B1, B2, B6, B12, folate, calcium, iron, zinc, iodine

Stuffed Provençal Tomatoes with Bulgar Wheat and Basil

Cost: £2.01
Serves 4

Serve this hot or at room temperature with the Leek and Thyme Vinaigrette and plenty of warm crusty bread to mop up the juices. If you're serving the tomatoes hot, top them with a little finely grated cheese if you like. You could also add a simple green salad.

90 g (3½ oz) bulgar wheat
4 large tomatoes
1 tbsp plus 2 tsp olive oil
1 red onion, finely chopped
1 tsp balsamic vinegar
6 pitted black olives, finely chopped
2 garlic cloves, crushed
2 tbsp shredded fresh basil
salt and freshly ground black pepper
basil sprigs, to garnish

1 Wash the bulgar wheat in several changes of cold water until the water becomes clear. Drain and put in a large bowl. Pour over enough boiling water to cover by about 2.5 cm (1 in). Leave to soak for at least 1 hour.

2 Using a very sharp knife, cut a thin slice from the top of each tomato. (Use the tops in another dish.) Cut around the inside edge of the tomatoes, taking care not to pierce the skin. Carefully scoop out the seeds and central ribs of flesh, leaving the outer shell intact. Drain the scooped out flesh and chop finely.

3 Heat 1 tbsp of the oil in a small frying pan. Add the onion and gently fry over a low heat for 15-20 minutes until very soft.

4 Drain the soaked bulgar wheat, pressing out as much liquid as possible with the back of a wooden spoon.

5 In a large bowl, mix together the bulgar wheat, onion, chopped tomato, vinegar, olives, garlic, shredded basil, and salt and pepper to taste.

6 Spoon the mixture into the prepared tomato shells, packing it in well and mounding the top. Place in a shallow baking dish into which the tomatoes will fit snugly. Drizzle the bulgar mixture with the remaining olive oil. Cover the top of each tomato with a circle of foil.

7 Bake in a preheated oven at 190°C/375°F/ Gas 5 for 30-40 minutes until the tomatoes are tender. Garnish with a basil leaf before serving.

Leek and Thyme Vinaigrette

Cost: £1.79
Serves 4

The new season's leeks should be making an appearance by now. Tender and full of flavour, they make a substantial salad.

700 g (1½ lb) small leeks, trimmed
2 tbsp olive oil
sea salt flakes
1 tsp balsamic vinegar
2 tsp chopped fresh thyme
1 tbsp chopped fresh flat-leafed
parsley
freshly ground black pepper
1 hard-boiled egg, chopped

1 Cut the leeks in half lengthways. Arrange in a single layer in a shallow baking tray into which they just fit. Sprinkle with the olive oil and sea salt to taste, turning to coat.

2 Roast in the top of a preheated oven at 240°C/475°F/Gas 9 for 10 minutes. Turn and roast for another 5-10 minutes until slightly blackened round the edges.

3 Allow to cool slightly, then slice crossways into 5 cm (2 in) pieces. Transfer to a serving bowl.

4 Toss with the vinegar, thyme, most of the parsley, and season with black pepper. Add more sea salt if necessary. Top with the chopped hard-boiled egg and sprinkle with the remaining parsley. Serve at room temperature.

Blackcurrant Tansy

Cost: £3.18
Serves 4

Shop-bought blackcurrants are expensive but a few go a long way. Bottled or canned ones are cheaper and almost as good in a dessert like this. Tansies are an old-fashioned dessert named after the pungent and bitter herb traditionally used to flavour them. They were usually made with custard, but low-fat fromage frais and whipped cream are a healthier and less time-consuming option.

**225 g (8 oz) blackcurrants, stalks removed
50 g (2 oz) caster sugar
150 ml (¼ pt) low-fat fromage frais
150 ml (¼ pt) whipping cream, whipped
blackcurrant or mint leaves, to decorate**

1 Put the blackcurrants in a small saucepan with 2 tbsp water. Cover and simmer for about 10 minutes until softened. Purée in a food processor or blender, then push through a sieve to remove the pips. You should have 150 ml (¼ pt) of purée.

2 Mix the purée with the sugar, stirring until completely dissolved. Set aside 3 tbsp of purée, and mix the rest with the fromage frais.

3 Fold in the whipped cream, then divide the mixture between 4 glass serving bowls. Chill until ready to serve. Swirl some of the reserved purée into each serving to give a marbled effect, and decorate with a blackcurrant or mint leaf.

NUTRITIONAL INFORMATION

First course per portion: calories 205 ●
protein 4g ● fat 9g ●
carbohydrate 26g ● fibre 2g ●
source of: iron, beta-carotene, folate, vitamins C, E

Main course per portion: calories 110 ●
protein 5g ● fat 8g ●
carbohydrate 5g ● fibre 4g ●
source of: iron, vitamins A, B, C, E

Dessert per portion: calories 225 ●
protein 4g ● fat 15g ●
carbohydrate 21g ● fibre 2g ●
source of: vitamins B12, A, C

SEPTEMBER

September is the month for enjoying the last of the summer treats, and looking ahead to more warming and sustaining food. As the first hint of evening chilliness makes itself felt, a slow-cooked casserole of lamb or pork, or richly stuffed vegetables, make welcome and economical dinners.

This is still the season of glut, so cooking for numbers becomes affordable. With the hedgerows bursting with berries and nuts, gardens and allotments at their peak, and market stalls and supermarkets piled high with harvest produce, there's plenty of scope for those with more dash than cash.

There are still plenty of summer salad greens and herbs, but they are coming to an end so prices should be good. Mediterranean vegetables are at their best and cheapest, and are delicious roasted or char-grilled. Tossed with pasta, they make a filling supper which won't break the bank.

Cauliflowers and sweetcorn are still good, but broad beans are finishing and should be a sensible price. You can perform culinary miracles on large, seemingly inedible, broad beans if you slip off the outer skins after boiling and whizz them in the blender with plenty of fresh herbs, cream cheese and seasoning.

This is the month for orchard fruit, glistening plums and blackberries, grapes and warm-scented melons. Prices should be reasonable, so treat yourself to some delicious fruit desserts.

BARGAIN FOOD IN SEASON

Vegetables

Aubergines ● Broad beans ● Cabbages ● Cauliflowers ● Courgettes ●
Cucumbers ● Green beans ● Herbs ● Peppers ● Salad greens ●
Sweetcorn ● Tomatoes

Fruit

Apples ● Blackberries ● Grapes ● Melons ● Pears ● Plums ● Soft fruit

1 Peel the kohlrabi and slice thinly. Stack a few slices at a time and cut into matchstick strips. Slice the cucumber and cut into matchstick strips in the same way. Cut the carrots into matchstick strips.

2 Mix the vegetables with the spinach or watercress and arrange attractively on individual plates.

3 Whisk the dressing ingredients until thick. Pour the dressing over the salad and sprinkle with the sunflower seeds. Serve at once.

MENU 1
Non-vegetarian
Total cost £6.27

•

Kohlrabi, Cucumber and Carrot Salad with Creamy Herb Dressing

•

Bacon and Bean Hotpot with Parsley Sauce

•

Baked Apples with Blackcurrants

Kohlrabi, Cucumber and Carrot Salad with Creamy Herb Dressing

Cost: £1.44
Serves 4

Choose small kohlrabi no bigger than a tennis ball. Larger specimens tend to have a woody texture. Their crisp flesh has a flavour somewhere between peppery radish and raw cabbage, and is a tasty addition to a winter salad.

2 kohlrabi
225 g (8 oz) cucumber, unpeeled
3 carrots
4 handfuls trimmed spinach or watercress, shredded
3 tbsp toasted sunflower seeds

DRESSING
1 tbsp wine vinegar
3 tbsp chopped fresh mixed herbs
salt and freshly ground black pepper
3 tbsp extra virgin olive oil
125 ml (4 fl oz) plain yogurt
2 tbsp soured cream

Bacon and Bean Hotpot with Parsley Sauce

Cost: £3.55
Serves 4

This is one of those old-fashioned homely dishes which never fail to please. Serve with steamed buttered cauliflower.

900 g (2 lb) piece gammon
175 g (6 oz) kidney beans
1 onion, chopped
1 carrot, chopped
bouquet garni
6 black peppercorns
2 sweetcorn ears

PARSLEY SAUCE
25 g (1 oz) butter
20 g (¾ oz) flour
200 ml (7 fl oz) ham stock
125 ml (4 fl oz) milk
2 tbsp finely chopped parsley
freshly ground black pepper

1 Soak the gammon and beans separately in cold water overnight. Drain both and rinse.

2 Put the beans in a saucepan and cover with fresh water. Bring to the boil, then continue to boil rapidly for 15 minutes. Drain and rinse.

3 Put the gammon in a heavy-based saucepan with the onion, carrot, bouquet garni, peppercorns and enough water to cover. Bring to the boil slowly and skim the surface of scum. Cover and simmer over a very low heat for 30 minutes. Add the beans and simmer for another 45 minutes.

4 Trim the kernels from the sweetcorn and add to the gammon for the last 15 minutes of cooking.

5 Remove the gammon and keep warm. Strain the stock and keep the beans and sweetcorn warm.

6 To make the sauce, melt the butter in a saucepan, add the flour and cook for 1 minute, stirring. Add the ham stock and whisk until smooth. Gradually whisk in the milk. Stir in the parsley and season with pepper.

7 Slice the gammon and serve with the beans, sweetcorn and the parsley sauce.

Baked Apples with Blackcurrants

Cost: £1.28
Serves 4

You could use blackberries instead of blackcurrants, especially if you've picked them yourself.

**4 cooking apples, cored
175 g (6 oz) blackcurrants
150 ml (¼ pt) water
5 tbsp clear honey
4 tbsp demerara sugar**

1 Score the apple skins around the middle. Put the apples into an ovenproof dish and fill the cavities with the blackcurrants.

2 Bring the water to the boil in a small saucepan. Stir in the honey until melted. Pour the mixture over the apples. Sprinkle with the sugar.

3 Bake in a preheated oven at 180°C/350F/Gas 4 for 45 minutes. Serve warm or cold.

NUTRITIONAL INFORMATION

First course per portion: calories 235 ●
protein 6g ● fat 17g ●
carbohydrate 14g ● fibre 5g ●
source of: fibre, calcium, thiamin,
vitamin C, beta-carotene

Main course per portion: calories 545 ●
protein 54g ● fat 24g ●
carbohydrate 28g ● fibre 6g ●
source of: iron, zinc,
B vitamins

Dessert per portion: calories 150 ●
protein 1g ● fat 0g ●
carbohydrate 39g ● fibre 4g ●
source of: vitamin C, fibre

Carrot, Fennel and Courgette Salad

Cost: £1.86
Serves 4

If fennel is too expensive, leave it out and use more courgettes and carrots instead. The vegetables need only minimal blanching – the colours should remain very bright.

2-3 carrots
1 large yellow courgette
1 large green courgette
1 fennel bulb
snipped fresh chives
small handful of toasted pumpkin seeds

DRESSING
2 tsp wine vinegar
¼ tsp Dijon mustard
salt and freshly ground black pepper
4 tbsp olive oil

1 Using a long sharp knife, cut the carrots and courgettes lengthways into 6 mm (¼ in) thick slices. Then cut each slice in half crossways.

2 Trim the fennel bulb and cut into quarters. Slice each quarter lengthways into thin slivers, still attached to the core.

3 Bring a large pan of water to the boil. Add the vegetables, bring back to the boil, then immediately drain under cold running water. Pat dry with paper towel.

4 Put the vegetables in a serving dish and toss with the chives and pumpkin seeds.

5 Whisk the dressing ingredients and pour over the vegetables. Leave to stand at room temperature for 30 minutes before serving.

Lamb Chop and Leek Casserole

Cost: £3.21
Serves 4

At around £1.50 a pound, frozen New Zealand lamb chops must be one of the best bargains around. However, they need tender loving care to bring out the best in them. A lengthy marinade and leisurely cooking are the answer, so start a day in advance.

MARINADE
2 tbsp olive oil
3 garlic cloves, very thinly sliced
finely grated zest of 1 lemon
2-3 rosemary sprigs
freshly ground black pepper

8 thin frozen New Zealand lamb chops, defrosted
250 g (9 oz) leeks, trimmed
450 g (1 lb) new potatoes, scrubbed
salt and freshly ground black pepper
1 tbsp olive oil
1 tbsp flour
200 ml (7 fl oz) stock
chopped parsley, to garnish

1 Combine the marinade ingredients. Lay the chops in a shallow dish into which they will fit in a single layer. Pour over the marinade, turning the chops to coat. Cover and leave in the fridge to marinate for at least 4 hours or preferably overnight.

2 Arrange the chops in a baking dish or roasting tin, overlapping them slightly. Cut the leeks in half lengthways, then slice them in half crossways. Tuck them in among the chops, together with the potatoes. Season with salt and a generous grinding of pepper, and drizzle a little oil over the leeks and potatoes.

3 Bake in a preheated oven at 190°C/375°F/Gas 5 for 1 hour, until the chops are tender. Move the chops and vegetables to a heated serving dish and keep warm.

4 Drain off all but 2 tbsp oil from the pan. Sprinkle with the flour and stir for a few seconds on top of the stove. Pour in the stock and stir in any crusty bits from the bottom of the dish. Strain over the chops and garnish with chopped parsley.

Spiced Compote of Fresh and Dried Orchard Fruits

Cost: £1.78
Serves 4

Use crisp eating apples such as Cox's, Russets or Discovery, preferably using free windfalls from your own garden or a friend's. Small pieces of dried fruit added to fresh fruit provide delicious bursts of flavour. You could try it the other way round and mix dried apples with fresh pears.

**700 g (1½ lb) crisp eating apples, quartered, cored and peeled
100 g (4 oz) dried pears, halved**

**450 ml (¾ pt) apple juice
2 tbsp clear honey
1 cinnamon stick, broken
6 cloves
seeds from 6 crushed cardamom pods
yogurt or fromage frais, to serve**

1 Put the apples and dried pear pieces in a saucepan with the remaining ingredients, except for the yogurt or fromage frais. Stir over a medium heat to dissolve the honey, then simmer for 8-10 minutes until the apples are tender but still hold their shape.

2 Serve warm or cold with yogurt or fromage frais.

NUTRITIONAL INFORMATION

First course per portion: calories 165 ● protein 3g ● fat 14g ● carbohydrate 8g ● fibre 4g ● source of: iron, vitamin B6, folate, beta-carotene, vitamin E

Main course per portion: calories 360 ● protein 31g ● fat 17g ● carbohydrate 23g ● fibre 3g ● source of: iron, zinc, vitamins B, C

Dessert per portion: calories 215 ● protein 4g ● fat 0g ● carbohydrate 53g ● fibre 5g ● source of: vitamins C, E

Broad Bean and Savory Pâté

Cost: £1.25
Serves 4

Summer savory is traditionally grown as a companion plant to broad beans to ward off blackfly. The flavour is perfect with the beans, but if you don't have any, use marjoram, thyme or oregano instead.

**275 g (10 oz) shelled small broad beans
grated zest of 1 lemon
50 g (2 oz) ricotta or cottage cheese
1 tbsp chopped summer savory
salt and freshly ground black pepper
toast, to serve**

1 Cook the beans in plenty of boiling water for about 3 minutes. Drain under cold running water and slip off the outer skins.
2 Purée with the lemon zest, ricotta, savory and seasoning. Spoon into a serving bowl, then cover and chill. Serve with hot toast.

Nut-Stuffed Red Cabbage with Tomato Sauce

Cost: £2.36
Serves 4

This is a spectacularly colourful dish with a crunchy stuffing. Serve with Grilled Tomato Sauce (47p, page 124).

**1 red cabbage
4 tbsp vegetable oil
100 g (4 oz) wholemeal breadcrumbs
100 g (4 oz) chopped mixed nuts
1 onion, finely chopped
2 carrots, grated
75 g (3 oz) mushrooms, chopped
2 garlic cloves, finely chopped
1 tbsp dried mixed herbs
finely grated zest of 1 lemon
salt and freshly ground black pepper
300 ml (½ pt) vegetable stock**

1 Peel away 6-8 outer leaves from the cabbage. Plunge the leaves into a large pan of boiling water for 2 minutes. Drain under cold running water and pat dry. Shave away the thickest part of the stalks.
2 Cut the centre of the cabbage in half. Discard one piece for another use. Cut the remaining piece in two and cut away the stalk. Slice the leaves crossways into thin shreds and set aside.
3 Heat half the oil in a frying pan and fry the breadcrumbs and nuts together until crisp. Transfer to a bowl and wipe the pan with paper towel.
4 Heat the remaining oil and fry the onion until translucent. Add the carrot, mushrooms, shredded cabbage, garlic and herbs. Gently fry for 7 minutes, then add to the nut mixture. Stir in the lemon zest, and season generously with salt and pepper. Stir in about half the stock - enough to bind the mixture.
5 Arrange the leaves around the edge of a shallow ovenproof round dish, overlapping them so there are no gaps, and allowing the tops of the leaves to hang over the edge of the bowl. Pile the stuffing in the middle and fold

over the tops of the leaves. Pour the remaining stock around the outside. Cover tightly with a double thickness of foil.

6 Bake in a preheated oven at 180°C/350°F/ Gas 4 for 45 minutes. Cut into wedges and serve with grilled tomato sauce.

Blackberry and Pear Crumble

Cost: £1.38
Serves 4

This delicious autumn pudding will cost you next to nothing with blackberries from the wild and windfall pears.

350 g (12 oz) blackberries
350 g (12 oz) cooking pears,
peeled, cored and sliced
pinch ground cinnamon
75 g (3 oz) sugar
175 g (6 oz) wholemeal flour
75 g (3 oz) butter
2 tbsp clear honey
finely grated zest of ½ lemon

1 Put the blackberries, pears, cinnamon and sugar in a 900 ml (1½ pt) ovenproof dish.

2 Put the flour in a bowl and gently rub in the butter. Stir in the honey and lemon zest, using a metal spoon.

3 Completely cover the fruit with the crumble topping. Bake in a preheated oven at 200°C/ 400°F/Gas 6 for 15 minutes, then at 190°C/ 375°F/Gas 5 for another 20-25 minutes until the topping is browned.

NUTRITIONAL INFORMATION

First course per portion: calories 80
● protein 6g ● fat 3g ●
carbohydrate 6g ● fibre 4g ●
source of: calcium, vitamin C, fibre

Main course per portion: calories 510
● protein 11g ● fat 39g ●
carbohydrate 30g ● fibre 8g ●
source of: calcium, iron,
B vitamins including folate, vitamin C,
beta-carotene, fibre

Dessert per portion: calories 425 ●
protein 7g ● fat 17g ●
carbohydrate 67g ● fibre 8g ●
source of: B vitamins,
fibre

MENU 4
Vegetarian
Total cost £6.95
●
Red Pepper Crostini
●
Stuffed Aubergines
●
Salad of Vine Fruits with Lime Cream

Red Pepper Crostini

Cost: £1.37
Serves 4

Soft strips of roasted pepper on crisp French bread make a simple starter. Try other roasted vegetables too; courgettes, mushrooms and aubergines are all delicious.

**2 red peppers
1 French stick
2 garlic cloves
olive oil
salt and freshly ground
black pepper**

1 Put the peppers in a roasting tin and roast in a preheated oven at 230°C/450°F/Gas 8 for 15-20 minutes, until the skin blackens and blisters. Turn the peppers frequently so that the skin chars evenly.

2 When the peppers are cool enough to handle, peel away the skin and remove the tops and seeds. Cut the flesh into thin strips.

3 Cut the French stick into about 12 slices. Rub with a cut clove of garlic and drizzle with olive oil. Place on a baking sheet and put in the oven for a few minutes until lightly toasted.

4 Pile the peppers on top, drizzle with a little more olive oil, season to taste and return to the oven for 3-4 minutes until heated through.

Stuffed Aubergines

Cost: £3.36
Serves 4

Choose plump aubergines which don't sound hollow when tapped. Serve with Grilled Tomato Sauce (47p, page 124) .

**4 aubergines
1 tbsp olive oil
1 onion, finely chopped
1 red pepper, finely diced
175 g (6 oz) cooked brown rice
(about 65 g/2½ oz uncooked)
100 g (4 oz) mushrooms, chopped
125 ml (4 fl oz) vegetable stock
salt and freshly ground
black pepper
50 g (2 oz) sunflower seeds
50 g (2 oz) Red Leicester cheese,
grated**

1 Prick the aubergines with a sharp knife, then bake in a preheated oven at 200°C/400°F/Gas 6 for 20-30 minutes until tender.

2 Meanwhile, heat the oil in a frying pan and gently fry the onion and pepper for a few minutes until soft. Stir in the rice, then add the mushrooms and stock. Season with salt and pepper, then cover and simmer over a low heat for 5 minutes, stirring occasionally.

3 Cut a lengthways slice from the top of each aubergine. Scoop out most of the flesh but leave enough behind so that they still hold their shape. Chop the flesh and add to the rice mixture, together with the sunflower seeds. Check the seasoning.

4 Pack the mixture into the aubergine shells, piling it up in the middle. Place in a greased baking dish and return to the oven for 15 minutes to heat through.

5 Top with the grated cheese and bake for another 3-5 minutes or brown under the grill.

Salad of Vine Fruits with Lime Cream

Cost: £2.22
Serves 4

Grapes are not the only fruit which grow on a vine – melons and kiwi fruit do too, and here they combine in a luscious fruit salad.

½ ripe melon
2 kiwi fruit
175 g (6 oz) green grapes
2 tbsp sugar, or to taste
juice and finely grated zest
of 2 limes
150 ml (¼ pt) whipping cream
4 small strawberries,
to decorate

1 Either chop the melon flesh into cubes or scoop it into balls with a melon baller. You will need about 150 g (5 oz). Put in a bowl.
2 Peel the kiwi fruit and thinly slice crossways, then cut into segments. Add to the melon in the bowl.
3 Halve the grapes and remove the seeds if necessary. Add to the fruit in the bowl, together with the sugar and two-thirds of the lime juice. Cover and chill.

4 Whip the cream until soft peaks form, then stir in half the lime zest and the remaining juice.
5 Divide the fruit among individual glass serving bowls. Spoon or pipe the cream over the top. Decorate with a strawberry and a sprinkling of the remaining lime zest.

NUTRITIONAL INFORMATION

First course per portion: calories 275
● protein 8g ● fat 8g ●
carbohydrate 47g ● fibre 2g ●
source of: calcium, iron, selenium,
vitamins A, C, E, folate

Main course per portion: calories 310
● protein 10g ● fat 18g ●
carbohydrate 28g ● fibre 6g ●
source of: calcium, iron,
zinc, selenium,
vitamins A, B, C, E

Dessert per portion: calories 240 ●
protein 2g ● fat 15g ●
carbohydrate 26g ● fibre 2g ●
source of: vitamins A, C

OCTOBER

Golden October is a time of shorter evenings, the first frosty nights and, if we're lucky, a few warm days of Indian summer. Orchards are laden with fruit – apples, pears, plums and quince – and, if the weather is kind, blackberries can be picked until mid-November.

It's a good time to make the most of Mediterranean vegetables such as courgettes, aubergines and peppers. Prices are particularly good in the autumn as the summer crop comes to an end. With the evenings drawing in, we can also start enjoying comforting casseroles and puddings of a more substantial nature.

The first nip of frost will see the end of the wild mushrooms, so make the most of them while you can. For me, a dish of freshly gathered mushrooms sautéed in butter and herbs represents something close to gastronomic euphoria, and the fact that they're free adds to the pleasure. If you have the good fortune to go on a 'funghi foray', make sure you can positively identify the mushrooms you have picked.

Also free for the asking are crisp crunchy cobnuts. Together with the new season's 'wet' walnuts, they are another early autumn treat. Eat them dipped in sea salt, or add to salads and fruit desserts.

Pumpkins appear in October and should not be relegated only to Halloween masks. Young firm specimens make a cheap and tasty vegetable dish when cubed and fried in good oil with spices and plenty of salt and pepper.

Root vegetables are also beginning to appear. They make cheap, nutritious and filling soups and casseroles. As a change from potatoes and parsnips, be adventurous and experiment with yams, sweet potatoes, celeriac and Jerusalem artichokes.

BARGAIN FOOD IN SEASON

Vegetables

Aubergines ● Cabbages ● Courgettes ● Garlic ● Leeks ● Peppers ●
Root vegetables ● Squash

Fruit

Apples ● Blackberries ● Grapes ● Pears ● Plums ● Quinces

Garlic Croûton Salad with Blue Cheese

Cost: £1.77
Serves 4

Use ciabatta, French bread or a day-old crusty white loaf for the croûtons. Don't remove the crusts.

7 tbsp olive oil
4 large garlic cloves, thinly sliced
4 thick slices slightly stale bread,
cut into 1 cm (½ in) cubes
1 large lettuce, washed and
thoroughly dried
1 tbsp finely chopped fresh
mixed herbs
lemon juice or wine vinegar, to taste
salt and freshly ground black pepper
100 g (4 oz) blue cheese, such as
gorgonzola or Bleu d'Auvergne,
crumbled

1 Heat 4 tbsp of the oil in a large frying pan. Add the garlic and fry over a medium-low heat for about 2 minutes until just beginning to colour. Do not allow the garlic to burn or it will taste bitter. Remove from the pan with a slotted spoon and set aside.

2 Raise the heat and add the bread cubes. Fry for about 5 minutes until golden brown on all sides. Remove from the pan and drain off the oil on paper towel.

3 Tear the lettuce into pieces and put in a salad bowl with the herbs. Add the remaining oil and toss gently until the leaves are coated. Sprinkle with a little lemon juice or wine vinegar, and season with salt and pepper.

4 Add the cheese, garlic and bread cubes. Toss again and serve at once.

Chicken, Celery and Mushroom Gougère with Walnuts

Cost: £2.96
Serves 4

This can be kept warm in the oven while you are eating the first course. If you haven't got four dishes, use one large one. Serve with stir-fried cabbage.

CHOUX PASTRY
75 g (3 oz) butter
200 ml (7 fl oz) water
¼ tsp salt
100 g (4 oz) plain flour, sifted
3 eggs, lightly beaten
40 g (1½ oz) Red Leicester cheese,
grated
1 tsp French mustard

FILLING
1 tbsp sunflower oil
25 g (1 oz) butter
200 g (7 oz) boneless, skinless chicken,
cut into bite-sized pieces
½ onion, finely chopped
4 small celery stalks, thinly sliced
75 g (3 oz) button mushrooms,
thinly sliced
2 tsp chopped fresh thyme or lovage
25 g (1 oz) plain flour
300 ml (½ pt) milk
2 tsp lemon juice
salt and freshly ground black pepper
50 g (2 oz) walnuts, toasted and
roughly chopped
celery leaves, to garnish

1 To make the choux pastry, put the butter, water and salt in a saucepan and stir over a gentle heat until the butter has melted. Bring just to the boil and remove from the heat.

2 Add the flour all at once and beat vigorously with a wooden spoon until the mixture pulls away from the sides of the pan. Beat for 1 minute over a very low heat until very smooth and glossy. Allow to cool slightly, then gradually beat in the eggs. Beat in the cheese and mustard.

3 Using a plain 1 cm (½ in) nozzle, pipe 2 circles of mixture, one on top of the other, around the edge of four 13 cm (5½ in) shallow ovenproof dishes. Bake in a preheated oven at 220°C/425°F/Gas 7 for about 25 minutes until golden and puffed.

4 While the pastry's cooking make the filling. Heat the oil and butter in a pan and fry the chicken for a few minutes until beginning to colour. Add the onion, celery, mushrooms and thyme, and gently fry until soft.

5 Add the flour and cook for 1 minute, stirring constantly. Remove from the heat, add the milk and bring to the boil, stirring constantly until thickened. Simmer over a very low heat for a few minutes. Add the lemon juice and season to taste. Stir in the walnuts.

6 Spoon into the centre of the choux rings. Garnish with celery leaves before serving.

Blackberry Jellies with Port

Cost: £1.51
Serves 4

To bring out the full flavour of the blackberries, allow the jellies to come to room temperature before serving.

**450 g (1 lb) blackberries
50 g (2 oz) sugar, or to taste
125 ml (4 fl oz) ruby port
1 sachet powdered gelatine
150 ml (¼ pint) whipping cream**

1 Put the blackberries and sugar in a saucepan with 150 ml (¼ pint) of water. Simmer over a low heat for about 10 minutes until the blackberries have softened and released their juice. Strain through a muslin-lined sieve into a measuring jug.

2 Add the port to the juice and enough water to make the mixture up to 600 ml (1 pint).

3 Warm 4 tbsp of the juice in a small pan. Remove from the heat. Sprinkle over the gelatine. Leave for 10 minutes to soften, then stir to dissolve. Warm gently if necessary to dissolve any large globules.

4 Stir the gelatine into the remaining juice. Pour into individual moulds or wine glasses. Chill for several hours until set.

5 Whip the cream until soft peaks form and spoon over the jellies just before serving.

NUTRITIONAL INFORMATION

First course per portion: calories 360 ● protein 8g ● fat 28g ● carbohydrate 18g ● fibre 1g ● source of: calcium, selenium, vitamins A, E, folate

Main course per portion: calories 605 ● protein 26g ● fat 43g ● carbohydrate 30g ● fibre 2g ● source of: calcium, iron, zinc, selenium, iodine, vitamins B1, B2, niacin, B6, B12, folate, vitamins A, E

Dessert per portion: calories 215 ● protein 5g ● fat 8g ● carbohydrate 24g ● fibre 3g ● source of: folate, vitamins A, C, E

Mushroom and Watercress Pâté

●

Herrings with Lemon and Rosemary

●

Pear Chocolate Roulade

Mushroom and Watercress Pâté

Cost: £1.25
Serves 4

This is a no-fuss first course with a nice peppery flavour from the watercress. It is even better if made with freshly gathered mushrooms.

50 g (2 oz) butter
1 onion, finely chopped
1 tsp coriander seeds, crushed
75 g (3 oz) mushrooms, finely chopped
40 g (1½ oz) trimmed watercress
100 g (4 oz) cottage cheese
Tabasco sauce
salt and freshly ground
black pepper

1 Melt the butter in a frying pan. Add the onion and coriander seeds, then gently fry for about 5 minutes until the onion is soft.
2 Raise the heat, add the mushrooms and stir-fry for a few minutes until most of the liquid has evaporated. Add the watercress and fry for 30 seconds, until just limp.
3 Tip the mixture into a food processor or blender. Add the cottage cheese, a few drops of Tabasco, and salt and pepper to taste.

Process until smooth, then pour into a serving bowl. Chill for 2-3 hours until firm. Serve with hot toast.

Herring with Lemon and Rosemary

Cost: £2.45
Serves 4

Oily fish such as herring or mackerel are always cheap and make a healthy alternative to meat. Serve these quickly cooked fillets with jacket potatoes and a selection of steamed green vegetables. Try thinly sliced leeks, celery, courgettes and shredded cabbage, or use whatever you have to hand. You'll only need a small amount of each.

1 tbsp flour
salt and freshly ground black pepper
4 x 175-225 g (6-8 oz) herring fillets
40 g (1½ oz) butter
finely grated zest and juice of 1 lemon
2 tsp finely chopped fresh rosemary
lemon wedges and rosemary
sprigs, to garnish

1 Mix the flour with the salt and pepper and use to dust the fillets.
2 Melt the butter in a large frying pan until foaming. Add the fillets and fry for 4-5 minutes, turning once. Add the lemon juice and rosemary and cook for another minute or two.
3 Transfer to a warm serving dish and garnish with lemon wedges and small sprigs of rosemary. Serve at once.

Pear Chocolate Roulade

Cost: £2.57
Serves 4

Eggs, flour and air make a cheap, filling dessert, so don't be put off by the length of the recipe. It is far less daunting than it appears, and can be prepared well ahead of time. If you are fortunate enough to have access to a quince tree, substitute a finely chopped quince for one of the pears. It will add a delicious fragrance to the filling.

flour, for sprinkling
3 eggs
75 g (3 oz) sugar
40 g (1½ oz) plain flour, less 1 tbsp
40 g (1½ oz) wholemeal flour
1 tbsp cocoa powder
icing sugar, for dusting
whipped cream or Greek yogurt,
to serve

FILLING
900 g (2 lb) ripe pears
1 tbsp sugar
thinly pared strip of orange peel
thinly pared strip of lemon peel
1 knob stem ginger, very finely
chopped

1 Lightly grease and line a 33 x 23 cm (13 x 9 in) Swiss roll tin with baking parchment. Sprinkle with flour and knock off any excess.

2 Using a hand-held electric beater, whisk the eggs and sugar in a large bowl until very thick and creamy. The mixture should leave a definite trail when the whisk is lifted. Sift the flours and cocoa powder over the surface, adding the bran from the wholemeal flour. Carefully fold in with a metal spoon.

3 Pour the mixture into the prepared tin, levelling and pushing the mixture into the corners with a palette knife. Bake in a preheated oven at 220°C/425°F/Gas 7 for 8-9 minutes until golden and springy to touch.

4 Turn out on to a sheet of lightly sugared greaseproof paper. Carefully peel off the baking parchment, then roll up from the narrow end, with the greaseproof paper still inside. Leave to cool.

5 Quarter, core, peel and slice the pears. Put in a saucepan with the sugar, citrus peels, ginger and 1 tbsp water. Cover and simmer over a low heat for 5 minutes, then uncover, raise the heat and simmer briskly for a further 10-15 minutes until most of the liquid has evaporated. The amount of time depends on how juicy your pears are. Be careful not to let the mixture burn. Remove from the heat, allow to cool, then fish out the citrus peel.

6 Unroll the cooked base and remove the greaseproof paper. Spread the filling over the surface, leaving a 1 cm (½ in) margin all round. Roll up carefully and place seam side down on a serving dish. Dust with icing sugar and serve with whipped cream or Greek yogurt.

NUTRITIONAL INFORMATION

First course per portion: calories 125 •
protein 4g • fat 11g •
carbohydrate 3g • fibre 1g •
source of: folate, vitamin A

Main course per portion: calories 395 •
protein 36g • fat 26g •
carbohydrate 3g • fibre 0g •
source of: calcium, iron, zinc,
selenium, iodine,
vitamins B group, E

Dessert per portion: calories 360 •
protein 11g • fat 9g •
carbohydrate 62g • fibre 7g •
source of: calcium, iron, zinc,
selenium, iodine,
vitamins B group, A, E

1 Put a large roasting tin in an oven preheated to 230°C/450°F/Gas 8.

2 Lightly brush the courgettes with oil. Arrange them cut side down in a single layer in the hot tin. Roast for 20-30 minutes, turning occasionally, until golden.

3 Cut the courgettes into 4 cm (1½ in) pieces. Put in a serving bowl and mix with the lemon zest, basil, olive oil and seasoning. Garnish with the olives. Leave to stand at room temperature for at least 1 hour to let the flavours develop.

4 Serve with warm ciabatta bread to mop up the juices.

Spicy Autumn Casserole with Pumpkin and Sweet Potato

Cost: £2.49
Serves 4

This can be prepared ahead of time up to the point where you add the cabbage. It freezes well and is worth making in quantity. Serve with rice or bulgar wheat.

1 tsp cumin seeds
2 tsp coriander seeds
1 tbsp sesame seeds
2 tsp dried oregano
2 tbsp vegetable oil
1 onion, chopped
3 garlic cloves, crushed
1-2 fresh red chillies, deseeded and chopped
225 g (8 oz) pumpkin, or 1 butternut squash, deseeded and cubed
2 sweet potatoes, cubed
3 carrots, thickly sliced
175 g (6 oz) green beans, chopped
400 g (14 oz) can chopped tomatoes
450 ml (12 fl oz) vegetable stock
salt and freshly ground black pepper
150 g (6 oz) shredded green cabbage

1 Put the seeds in a small, heavy-based pan without any oil. Heat until the aroma rises. Add the oregano and dry-fry for a few more seconds. Remove from the heat and crush with a pestle and mortar.

Roasted Courgette, Lemon and Basil Salad

Cost: £2.20
Serves 4

If you have that old-fashioned herb lovage growing in your garden, use it instead of basil. It is a really good combination with the lemon. Leave some space between the courgette slices when you roast them, otherwise they tend to cook in their own steam rather than browning nicely. Serve at room temperature with plenty of crusty bread to mop up the juices.

8 small courgettes, trimmed and sliced lengthways into 4 segments
oil for brushing
finely grated zest of ½ lemon
6 basil leaves, torn
3 tbsp extra virgin olive oil
salt and freshly ground black pepper
4-6 pitted black olives, to garnish
warm ciabatta bread, to serve

2 Heat the oil in a heavy-based casserole and gently fry the onion for a few minutes until translucent. Add the garlic and chillies and fry for 3 minutes more until soft. Stir in the seed mixture, then add the pumpkin, sweet potatoes, carrots and beans. Cook for 3-4 minutes more.

3 Next, add the tomatoes, stock and seasoning. Bring to the boil, then cover and simmer for 45 minutes, moistening with more stock if necessary.

4 A few minutes before serving, stir in the cabbage and cook until just wilted but still crunchy.

Plum Compote with Honey and Ginger

Cost: £1.98
Serves 4

425 ml (¾ pt) water
4 tbsp clear honey, or to taste
2 knobs stem ginger, chopped
450 g (1 lb) plums, halved and stoned
50 g (2 oz) flaked almonds, toasted
fromage frais or Greek yogurt, to serve

1 Put the water, honey and ginger in a saucepan and heat gently until the honey is dissolved.

2 Add the prepared plums and simmer for 8-12 minutes until tender.

3 Transfer the plums to a serving dish. Boil down the poaching liquid until syrupy and pour over the plums.

4 Sprinkle with the almonds and serve warm or cold, with fromage frais or yogurt.

NUTRITIONAL INFORMATION

First course per portion: calories 120 ●
protein 2g ● fat 12g ●
carbohydrate 2g ● fibre 1g ●
source of: folate,
vitamins A, C, E

Main course per portion: calories 370 ●
protein 7g ● fat 8g ●
carbohydrate 67g ● fibre 6g ●
source of: calcium, iron, vitamin B1,
folate, beta-carotene,
vitamins C, E

Dessert per portion: calories 230 ●
protein 7g ● fat 11g ●
carbohydrate 28g ● fibre 3g ●
source of: calcium,
vitamins B2, B12, E, A

MENU 4

Vegetarian

Total cost £6.02

•

Spinach, Egg and Walnut Salad

•

Mushroom and Shallot Sauté with Polenta

•

Coconut Rice Pudding with Pomegranates and Lemon Syrup

Spinach, Egg and Walnut Salad

Cost: £1.63
Serves 4

The price of spinach varies widely, so look for bargains. I have bought it for as little as 45p/lb in my local market, while spinach sold in supermarkets can be three times the price. Use freshly gathered cobnuts instead of walnuts if you like.

225 g (8 oz) tender spinach
4 spring onions, sliced
1 small red pepper, deseeded and very thinly sliced
3 tbsp chopped fresh chives
40 g (1½ oz) walnuts, roughly chopped
salt and freshly ground black pepper
3-4 tbsp olive oil
2 tsp balsamic vinegar
3 hard-boiled eggs, sliced

1 Remove the spinach stalks and tear the leaves into bite-sized pieces. Put the spinach in a salad bowl with the onions, red pepper, and most of the chives and walnuts.

2 Season with salt and pepper, then pour over enough oil to just coat the leaves. Toss gently, then sprinkle with the vinegar and toss again.
3 Arrange the eggs on top and sprinkle with the rest of the chives and walnuts. Serve at once.

Mushroom and Shallot Sauté with Polenta

Cost: £2.68
Serves 4

This is a grown-up version of mushrooms on toast, best of all made with mushrooms which you have gathered yourself – but be sure you can positively identify them. Otherwise, buy your mushrooms from a greengrocer or market selling local produce; they'll be cheaper than the supermarket. Serve with frozen broad beans cooked for about 3 minutes in a large pot of boiling water, or steamed wedges of Savoy cabbage.

175 g (6 oz) polenta (yellow cornmeal)
½ tsp salt
olive oil, for brushing
50 g (2 oz) butter
4 tbsp olive oil
4 tbsp chopped fresh sage
175 g (6 oz) shallots or baby onions
salt and freshly ground black pepper
600 g (1¼ lb) assorted mushrooms, such as large flat cap, chestnut or field mushrooms, cut into bite-sized chunks
squeeze of lemon juice
cayenne pepper
parsley, to garnish

1 Put the polenta and salt in a large saucepan with 1 L (1¾ pt) cold water. Bring to the boil, stirring. Simmer for 15-20 minutes, continuing to stir, until the mixture is smooth and starts to come away from the sides of the pan.
2 Pour into a 30 x 24 cm (12 x 9 in) Swiss roll tin, pushing the mixture into the corners and levelling the surface. Leave to cool, then cut into rectangles.

3 Brush the polenta with oil on both sides and spread out in a roasting tin. Place under a preheated grill or in a very hot oven for about 10 minutes, turning once, until golden and crisp. Keep warm while you cook the vegetables.

4 Heat 15 g (½ oz) of the butter and 1 tbsp of the oil in a small pan. Add 1 tbsp of the sage and fry for a few seconds to flavour the oil. Add the shallots and fry over a medium heat for 4-5 minutes until beginning to colour. Season to taste, then cover and leave to fry gently over a low heat while you cook the mushrooms.

5 Heat the remaining butter and oil in a large pan. Add the rest of the sage and fry for a few seconds. Add the mushrooms and stir-fry over a medium-high heat for 5-7 minutes until some of the liquid has evaporated.

6 Add the shallots and their juices to the mushrooms. Season generously with salt and pepper, a squeeze of lemon and a dash of cayenne.

7 To serve, place 2-3 pieces of polenta on each plate, top with the mushroom mixture and garnish with parsley.

Coconut Rice Pudding with Pomegranates and Lemon Syrup

Cost: £1.71
Serves 4

If your idea of rice pudding is coloured by memories of school dinners, just try this. You can use short-grain pudding rice, soaked for 1 hour, instead of Thai Fragrant rice. If pomegranates are unavailable, top the pudding with a few dried cranberries instead.

100 g (4 oz) Thai Fragrant rice,
well washed
350 ml (12 fl oz) water
850 ml (1½ pt) milk
3 tbsp coconut milk powder
seeds from 2 cardamom pods,
crushed
40 g (1½ oz) sugar
seeds from 1 pomegranate

SYRUP
100 g (4 oz) sugar, preferably
golden granulated
125 ml (4 fl oz) water
1½ tbsp lemon juice

1 Put the rice and water in a saucepan, bring to the boil, then cover and simmer over a very low heat for 15 minutes until the water is absorbed.

2 Stir in the milk, coconut powder and cardamom seeds. Partially cover and cook gently for 1¼-1½ hours until thick and creamy, stirring occasionally and then more frequently towards the end of cooking time to prevent sticking.

3 Stir in the sugar, then pour into a bowl and scatter the pomegranate seeds over the top.

4 To make the syrup, dissolve the sugar in the water and lemon juice over a medium heat. Boil hard for 7-10 minutes until syrupy. Pour over the rice and then serve warm, or at room temperature.

NUTRITIONAL INFORMATION

First course per portion: calories 235 ●
protein 8g ● fat 21g ●
carbohydrate 4g ● fibre 2g ●
source of: calcium, iron, zinc, iodine,
vitamins A, B group, C, E

Main course per portion: calories 385 ●
protein 7g ● fat 25g ●
carbohydrate 33g ● fibre 3g ●
source of: iron, zinc, folate,
vitamins A, C

Dessert per portion: calories 350 ●
protein 9g ● fat 4g ●
carbohydrate 74g ● fibre 1g ●
source of: calcium, zinc, iodine,
vitamins B group

NOVEMBER

As the clocks go back, November can seem a dispiriting month, but it is also a time when the markets are bursting with good cheap winter staples, and we get a hint of Christmas with the arrival of the new season's nuts, clementines and satsumas. Dried fruits come into their own at this time of year. They make delicious healthy desserts and are economical too, as a few go a long way.

November is the month for enjoying leisurely cooked casseroles, hearty soups and mellow flavours. Breast of lamb, shin of beef, heart or pork belly are all economical cuts which respond well to such treatment. Dried pulses and earthy root vegetables are the ideal accompaniment for mopping up delicious gravies, while vibrant cabbages provide freshness and colour.

Freshly gathered chestnuts, walnuts and cobnuts are a delight with their fresh, sweet flavour and crunchy texture. Add them to stuffings, salads and desserts. Apples, pears and fragrant quinces are also very good at this time of year, and make delicious tarts and pies.

If you don't have access to free supplies of these autumnal goodies, look for them in local markets or greengrocers – you'll often find local produce at reasonable prices.

BARGAIN FOOD IN SEASON

Vegetables

Beetroot ● Cabbages ● Carrots ● Cauliflowers ● Leeks ●
Mushrooms ● Squash ● Root vegetables

Fruit

Apples ● Citrus fruit ● Pears ● Quinces

1 Put the peppers on a baking tray and roast in a preheated oven at 230°C/450°F/Gas 8 for 15-20 minutes, turning frequently, until the skin blackens. Allow to cool, then peel off the skin and remove the seeds. Chop the flesh into 2 cm (¾ in) squares.

2 In a large bowl, combine the peppers, beetroot, cabbage, onion, chilli, garlic and herbs. Toss with just enough olive oil to coat. Sprinkle with a few drops of balsamic vinegar and season to taste.

3 Arrange the frisée on individual plates with the vegetable mixture in the middle. Take care to place the mixture exactly where you want it, otherwise the beetroot juice will stain the green leaves. Sprinkle with a few pumpkin seeds and serve at once.

Braised Ox Heart with Walnut and Orange Stuffing

Cost: £3.22
Serves 4

Don't be put off by ox heart – it is not as unpromising as it sounds. It has a pleasantly mild flavour, and it is one of the cheapest meats around. Ox heart is low in fat too, and extremely rich in iron and B vitamins. Serve with Parsnip and Sesame Purée (59p, page 119) and buttered kale.

900 g (2 lb) ox heart
2 tbsp vinegar
2 tbsp vegetable oil
3 tbsp flour, seasoned with salt,
pepper and cayenne
300 ml (½ pt) good beef stock
3 carrots, sliced
chopped parsley, to garnish

STUFFING
75 g (3 oz) fresh breadcrumbs
25 g (1 oz) walnuts, roughly
chopped
1 celery stalk, finely diced
2 garlic cloves, finely chopped
3 tbsp chopped fresh mixed herbs,
such as parsley, rosemary, thyme
finely grated zest of 1 orange

Red Vegetable Salad

Cost: £2.27
Serves 4

This technicolour vitamin-packed salad is full of delicious flavours – the slightly bitter frisée and peppery red cabbage contrasting with the sweetish beetroot and red pepper.

2 red peppers
3 small fresh beetroot, peeled and
coarsely grated
175 g (6 oz) shredded red cabbage
½ red onion, very thinly sliced
into rings
1 fresh red chilli, deseeded and
finely chopped
1 garlic clove, very finely chopped
4 tbsp chopped fresh mixed herbs
extra virgin olive oil
few drops balsamic vinegar
salt and freshly ground black pepper
1 head of frisée or escarole, torn
into bite-sized pieces
toasted pumpkin seeds, to
garnish

1 tbsp orange juice
1 tsp green peppercorns, crushed
½ tsp salt
beaten egg, to bind

1 Put the heart in a bowl and cover with cold water. Add the vinegar and leave to soak for 3 hours or overnight. Drain and pat dry. Cut through the flesh adjoining the cavities so that the heart lies flat in one piece. Cut away any veins and tubes.

2 Combine the stuffing ingredients and spread over the heart. Roll up and seal the edges with a needle and coarse thread.

3 Heat the oil in a small casserole which will hold the heart snugly. Coat the heart with seasoned flour and brown on all sides.

4 Pour in the stock and bring to the boil. Cover tightly and move to an oven preheated to 150°C/300°F/Gas 2. Cook for 2 hours, then add the carrots and cook for another hour.

5 Transfer the heart to a warm serving dish and remove the thread. Carve into slices and pour over the sauce. Garnish with parsley and serve at once.

Quince Compote

Cost: 33p (using pick-your-own quinces)
Serves 4

This is a bargain dessert if you're lucky enough to have your own quince tree, or can beg some windfalls from a neighbour. You can also buy quinces in shops selling Middle Eastern or Spanish produce, but they are not always cheap. Otherwise, use conference pears or a mixture of pears and quinces.

3 large quinces, quartered, cored,
   peeled and sliced lengthways
200 g (7 oz) sugar
seeds from 6 cardamom pods
2 strips orange peel
chopped stem ginger, to garnish

1 Put the prepared quinces, sugar, cardamom seeds and orange peel in a pan with just enough water to cover. Bring to the boil, stirring to dissolve the sugar. Cover and simmer over a low heat for about 1 hour until the quinces are soft and have turned a rosy pink.

2 Remove the orange peel and transfer the quinces to a bowl. Serve warm or chilled, garnished with stem ginger. Add a little of the syrup from the ginger jar if you like.

NUTRITIONAL INFORMATION

First course per portion: calories 125 ●
protein 3g ● fat 7g ●
carbohydrate 12g ● fibre 4g ●
source of: iron, beta-carotene, folate,
vitamins C, E

Main course per portion: calories 490 ●
protein 49g ● fat 20g ●
carbohydrate 30g ● fibre 3g ●
source of: iron, zinc,
vitamins B group, A, C, E

Dessert per portion: calories 245 ●
protein 0g ● fat 0g ●
carbohydrate 64g ● fibre 2g ●
source of: vitamin C

MENU 2
Non-vegetarian
Total cost £6.24

●

**Warm Vegetable Salad with
Mustard Dressing**

●

Sausage and Bean Hotpot

●

**Banana and Cardamom
Soufflé**

1 Peel the artichokes and slice thickly. To prevent browning, drop them into a bowl of water to which you have added some lemon juice.
2 Peel the kohlrabi and slice horizontally into 6mm (¼ in) slices. Stack the slices, cut them in half and then into thin strips.
3 Trim the broccoli where the head meets the stalk. Slice the stalks neatly (they can go into the salad as well). Trim the florets so that they are no more than 2.5 cm (1 in) across.
4 Drain the artichokes and put in a steamer basket with the kohlrabi. Arrange the broccoli on top. Steam over boiling water for 4-5 minutes until only just tender.
5 Whisk the dressing ingredients until thick.
6 Put the vegetables in a serving bowl and pour over the dressing. Toss gently and add the hazelnuts and parsley. Serve while still warm.

Warm Vegetable Salad with Mustard Dressing

Cost: £1.65
Serves 4

If you prefer, use different vegetables for this dish. Try celeriac or thinly sliced parsnip instead of Jerusalem artichokes, or even potatoes as long as they are not too floury. Or use cauliflower instead of broccoli, adding some carrot for colour. If you don't have a steamer, use a colander suspended over a pan of boiling water, with a lid on top.

350 g (12 oz) Jerusalem artichokes
lemon juice
1 medium kohlrabi
100 g (4 oz) broccoli florets
50 g (2 oz) shelled hazelnuts,
toasted and roughly chopped
2 tbsp chopped fresh parsley
or chives

DRESSING
1½ tbsp Dijon mustard
1 tbsp wine vinegar
salt and freshly ground
black pepper
4 tbsp extra virgin olive oil

Sausage and Bean Hotpot

Cost: £3.24
Serves 4

Use a mixture of sausages such as good quality butcher-made pork sausages, frankfurters, spicy chorizo and Polish sausage. This needs no accompaniment except some good crusty bread to mop up the juices. It improves with reheating.

175 g (6 oz) haricot beans, soaked
overnight
175 g (6 oz) black turtle or kidney
beans, soaked overnight
1 tsp cumin seeds
2 tsp coriander seeds
2 tsp dried oregano
2 tbsp vegetable oil
450 g (1 lb) mixed sausages
and salami, thickly sliced diagonally
1 onion, chopped
3 garlic cloves, finely chopped
400 g (14 oz) can chopped tomatoes
2 tbsp tomato purée
850 ml (1½ pt) chicken, beef
or ham stock
salt and freshly ground black pepper
3 tbsp chopped fresh flat-leafed parsley

1 Drain the beans, put in separate saucepans and cover with fresh water. Bring to the boil and boil rapidly for 15 minutes. Drain and set aside.

2 Toast the cumin and coriander seeds in a small, heavy-based pan over medium heat, without adding any oil. Add the oregano and toast for another 10 seconds until fragrant. Remove from the pan. Lightly crush the mixture with a pestle and mortar.

3 Heat the oil in a large, heavy-based saucepan or casserole. Add the sausages and salami, and fry for about 5 minutes until browned. Remove with a slotted spoon.

4 Add the onion to the pan, and fry for a few minutes until pale golden. Add the garlic and fry for another minute. Add the sausages, beans, spice mixture, tomatoes, tomato purée, and stock.

5 Stir well, bring to the boil, then cover and simmer over a gentle heat for 1½-2 hours until the beans are very tender. The mixture should be wet but not too sloppy. If there is too much liquid, remove the cover and simmer for 5 minutes until reduced. Season to taste and stir in the parsley. Go easy on the salt – sausages can be very salty.

Banana and Cardamom Soufflé

Cost: £1.35
Serves 4

The humble banana is often overlooked when it comes to desserts. They are cheap, adaptable and delicious, especially when warm. Here they make an impressive soufflé which will undoubtedly sink as it cools but is none the worse for it.

sugar, for dusting
3 large bananas
juice and finely grated zest of 1 lemon
50 g (2 oz) sugar
1 tbsp cornflour
crushed seeds from 6 green
cardamom pods
pinch of salt
175 ml (6 fl oz) semi-skimmed milk
3 eggs, separated
25 g (1 oz) butter, melted

1 Lightly grease a 1.5 L (2½ pt) soufflé dish or ovenproof bowl. Dust with sugar, tipping out the excess.

2 Slice the bananas and purée in a blender with the lemon juice until creamy.

3 Combine the lemon zest, sugar, cornflour, cardamom and salt in a small bowl. Stir in a little of the milk and blend to a smooth paste.

4 Scald the rest of the milk and mix it with the cornflour mixture. Return to the pan and cook over a gentle heat for 2-3 minutes, stirring constantly, until thickened. Remove from the heat.

5 Beat the egg yolks in a large bowl. Gradually add the hot sauce, beating well between each addition. Beat in the butter, followed by the banana purée.

6 Whisk the egg whites until stiff but not dry. Fold about one-third into the banana mixture to slacken it, then carefully fold in the rest.

7 Pour into the prepared dish. Bake in a preheated oven at 170°C/325°F/Gas 3 for 55-60 minutes until well risen and golden. Serve immediately.

NUTRITIONAL INFORMATION

First course per portion: calories 245 ●
protein 6g ● fat 20g ●
carbohydrate 13g ● fibre 6g ●
source of: iron, folate, vitamins C, E

Main course per portion: calories 685 ●
protein 33g ● fat 39g ●
carbohydrate 53g ● fibre 16g ●
source of: calcium, iron, zinc,
selenium, vitamins B, A, C, E

Dessert per portion: calories 270 ●
protein 9g ● fat 11g ●
carbohydrate 36g ● fibre 1g ●
source of: iron, iodine, vitamins A,
B group

MENU 3
Vegetarian
Total cost £4.91
●
Chestnut and Squash Soup
●
Stuffed Cabbage Leaves with
Lemon and Dill
●
Caramel Clementines with
Dates and Pistachio Nuts

1 Put the squash in a saucepan with 300 ml (½ pt) of water. Bring to the boil, cover and simmer for 15 minutes, then drain.

2 Melt the butter in a saucepan. Add the onion and celery, cover, and cook for 5 minutes. Add the squash, prepared chestnuts, orange peel, stock, salt, pepper and ginger. Bring to the boil, then cover and simmer for 30 minutes. Discard the orange peel.

3 Tip the soup into a food processor or blender, and purée until smooth. Return to the pan and add the orange juice. Reheat and check the seasoning.

4 Garnish each serving with celery leaves and a little chopped chestnut.

Stuffed Cabbage Leaves with Lemon and Dill

Cost: £1.17
Serves 4

Dill goes well with cabbage and adds an Eastern European touch. If it's hard to find, use parsley instead. Lemon zest and juice add a lovely sharpness and lightness to what can sometimes be a heavy dish. Serve with steamed carrots.

100 g (4 oz) long-grain brown rice
1½ tsp salt
6 large Savoy cabbage leaves
2 tbsp grated onion
50 g (2 oz) grated carrot
1 tsp finely grated lemon zest
¼ tsp freshly ground black pepper
1 egg, lightly beaten
300-425 ml (½-¾ pt) vegetable stock
75 g (3 oz) butter
2 tsp lemon juice
½ tsp dill seeds, or 2 tsp chopped fresh dill

1 Wash the rice, then put in a saucepan with 1 tsp of salt and enough water to cover by the depth of your thumb-nail. Bring to the boil, stir once, then cover tightly and simmer over very low heat for 40 minutes until the water has been absorbed. Fluff with a fork and leave to cool.

Chestnut and Squash Soup

Cost: £1.46
Serves 4

If using dried chestnuts, soak them overnight, simmer in fresh water for 1½ hours, then drain. If using fresh chestnuts, peel, husk and boil them until tender. Drain and use as in the recipe.

350 g (12 oz) butternut squash
or pumpkin, peeled and cut
into chunks
50 g (2 oz) butter or sunflower
margarine
1 onion, chopped
2 celery sticks, leaves included,
chopped
75 g (3 oz) dried chestnuts or
350 g (12 oz) fresh chestnuts
2 strips of orange peel (without pith)
600 ml (1 pt) vegetable stock
1 tsp salt
½ tsp freshly ground black pepper
½ tsp ground ginger
100 ml (3½ fl oz) orange juice
chopped celery leaves, to garnish
chopped chestnuts, to garnish

2 Blanch the cabbage leaves in boiling water for 2 minutes. Drain and pat dry. With a sharp knife, shave away the thickest part of the stalk so that the leaves are easier to roll.

3 Combine the rice, onion, carrot, lemon zest, pepper and remaining salt, then mix in the beaten egg.

4 Divide the stuffing between the leaves. Fold over the bottom, then the sides of each leaf and roll into a neat parcel.

5 Place the parcels seam-side down in single layer in a greased shallow casserole. They should fit quite snugly. Pour in about 300 ml (½ pt) of the stock and dot with a little of the butter. Cover and bake in a preheated oven at 180°C/350°F/Gas 4 for 30-35 minutes until the leaves are tender. Add more stock if necessary. Remove the lid and bake for 10 minutes more.

6 Heat the remaining butter in a small saucepan with the lemon juice and dill. Whisk until slightly thickened. Pour over the parcels and serve at once.

Caramel Clementines with Dates and Pistachio Nuts

Cost: £2.28
Serves 4

Use satsumas instead of clementines if they are cheaper. There is no need to remove the membrane if it is not tough.

75 g (3 oz) sugar
200 ml (7 fl oz) water
10 clementines
25 g (1 oz) shelled pistachio nuts
**50 g (2 oz) fresh dates, cut
into slivers**

1 Put the sugar in a small, heavy-based saucepan over a gentle heat. When the sugar has melted and turned golden remove from the heat and add the water. When the spluttering has died down, return the pan to the heat and stir until any lumps have dissolved. Leave to cool, then stir in the strained juice of two of the clementines.

2 Peel the remaining clementines. Using a very sharp knife and working over a bowl to catch the juice, cut down between the membrane and flesh of each segment. Ease out the flesh and put in a serving bowl with the caramel and the juice.

3 Cover the pistachios with boiling water. Leave for 5 minutes, then slip off the skins.

4 Add the pistachios and dates to the clementines. Chill before serving.

NUTRITIONAL INFORMATION

First course per portion: calories 200 ● protein 2g ● fat 12g ● carbohydrate 24g ● fibre 3g ● source of: iron, folate, vitamins A, C, E

Main course per portion: calories 265 ● protein 4g ● fat 18g ● carbohydrate 23g ● fibre 2g ● source of: iodine, B12, folate, beta-carotene, vitamin C

Dessert per portion: calories 180 ● protein 3g ● fat 4g ● carbohydrate 37g ● fibre 3g ● source of: vitamin C, folate

MENU 4
Vegetarian
Total cost £6.21

●

Black Bean and Red Pepper Soup

●

Spiced Pumpkin, Peanut and Green Bean Stir-fry

●

Dried Apricot and Sweet Couscous Pudding

1 Drain the beans and put in a saucepan with enough fresh water to cover. Bring to the boil, then boil rapidly for 15 minutes. Drain and set aside.

2 Heat the oil in a large, heavy-based saucepan. Add the herbs and cook for 30 seconds to flavour the oil. Add the onion, celery, red pepper, black peppercorns and coriander seeds. Gently fry for 5 minutes until the onion is translucent. Add the garlic, then cover and cook over a medium-low heat for another 5 minutes.

3 Next, add the beans, tomatoes, and 600 ml (1 pt) of stock. Bring to the boil, then cover and simmer over a low heat for 1 hour, until the beans are soft, stirring occasionally.

4 Fish out the bay leaves, then purée two-thirds of the mixture in a food processor (or all of it if you prefer a completely smooth soup). Return to the pan and reheat. Thin with the remaining stock if necessary, but the soup should be fairly thick.

5 Add the salt and lemon juice. Garnish each serving with a swirl of yogurt.

Black Bean and Red Pepper Soup

Cost: £1.30
Serves 4

This is a heartwarming, gutsy soup which is almost a meal in itself.

175 g (6 oz) black turtle beans, soaked overnight
2 tbsp vegetable oil
2 bay leaves
2 small sprigs fresh rosemary or thyme
1 onion, finely chopped
2 celery stalks, finely diced
1 red pepper, deseeded and finely diced
1 tsp black peppercorns, crushed
1 tsp coriander seeds, toasted and crushed
2 garlic cloves, finely chopped
200 g (7 oz) can chopped tomatoes
600-850 ml (1-1½ pt) vegetable stock
½ tsp salt
2 tbsp lemon juice
2 tbsp plain yogurt, to garnish

Spiced Pumpkin, Peanut and Green Bean Stir-fry

Cost: £2.35
Serves 4

Don't worry if you don't have all the spices, make do with whatever you have to hand. You can buy asafoetida in Asian stores. It smells unpleasant when raw, but cooking transforms it to a beautiful mellow flavour something like a mixture of onions and mushrooms. This can be made in advance and gently reheated. Serve with plainly boiled rice or bulgar wheat.

350 g (¾ lb) stringless green beans, cut into 4 cm (1½ in) pieces
4 tbsp vegetable oil
2 dried red chillies, deseeded
½ tsp black mustard seeds
½ tsp cumin seeds
½ tsp asafoetida (optional)
1 tsp salt

½ tsp sugar
½ tsp ground turmeric
¼ tsp garam masala
450 g (1 lb) pumpkin, peeled,
deseeded and cut into 2 cm
(¾ in) cubes
50 g (2 oz) peanuts, roughly
chopped
200 g (7 oz) can chopped
tomatoes

1 Plunge the beans into a large pan of boiling water. Bring back to the boil, then boil for 1 minute. Drain under cold running water. Pat dry with paper towel and set aside.
2 Heat the oil in a large saucepan. Add the chillies, mustard and cumin seeds, and asafoetida, if using. When the mustard seeds begin to pop, add the salt, sugar, turmeric and garam masala. Stir-fry for 30 seconds.
3 Add the pumpkin and stir-fry over a medium-high heat for 5 minutes until beginning to brown. Stir in the beans and peanuts. Cover and cook over a low heat for 3-5 minutes until tender, stirring occasionally.
4 Stir in the chopped tomato and cook for 5 more minutes.

Dried Apricot and Sweet Couscous Pudding

Cost: £2.56
Serves 4

Serve this warm or at room temperature. You can make the couscous the day before. If you don't have any dried cherries, use raisins instead.

150 g (5 oz) couscous
100 g (4 oz) dried apricots,
halved lengthways
75 g (3 oz) sugar
piece of cinnamon stick
juice and finely grated zest of
½ lemon
50 g (2 oz) butter
50 g (2 oz) dried sour cherries
25 g (1 oz) flaked almonds
150 ml (¼ pt) thin cream

1 Put the couscous in a shallow dish. Add enough cold water to cover by 2.5 cm (1 in) and leave to soak for 1 hour. Put in a fine sieve and press out any remaining moisture with the back of a wooden spoon.
2 Meanwhile, put the apricots in a saucepan with 425 ml (¾ pt) water, the sugar, cinnamon, and lemon juice and zest. Bring to the boil, then simmer for 15-20 minutes until the juices start to look syrupy. Strain, reserving the juice and set aside.
3 Heat the butter in a frying pan. Add the cherries and almonds and stir-fry for 2 minutes until the almonds are golden. Be careful not to let them burn. Add the couscous, stirring constantly, then add the cream. Cook gently for a few more minutes until heated through.
4 Tightly pack the couscous mixture into 4 lightly greased ramekins. Turn out on to individual plates and surround with the apricots. Pour the apricot juice over the couscous.

NUTRITIONAL INFORMATION

First course per portion: calories 225 ●
protein 12g ● fat 7g ●
carbohydrate 32g ●
fibre 5g ● source of: calcium,
iron, zinc, vitamins A, B1, B6, C,
folate

Main course per portion: calories 215 ●
protein 6g ● fat 18g ●
carbohydrate 9g ● fibre 4g ●
source of: iron, vitamins A, B1, B6,
C, E, folate

Dessert per portion: calories 420 ●
protein 6g ● fat 21g ●
carbohydrate 54g ● fibre 3g ●
source of: iron, vitamins A, E

DECEMBER

As the festive season draws near, there is an enormous choice of both familiar and exotic foods: gleaming tangerines, rosy apples, jewel-like pomegranates and Sharon fruit, baskets of nuts and dried fruit, creamy Stiltons, smoked salmon and game.

However, if you are budget- and health-conscious, simple but tasty dishes are often very welcome before the Christmas festivities begin. Soups, gratins, grilled chicken, rice, lightly cooked vegetables and refreshing fruit desserts are not only easy on the purse, but quick to prepare at this hectic time of year.

BARGAIN FOOD IN SEASON

Vegetables

Brussels sprouts ● Cabbages ● Carrots ● Celeriac ● Jerusalem artichokes ●
Leeks ● Parsnips ● Swedes

Fruit

Apples ● Bananas ● Citrus fruit ● Dried fruit ● Nuts ● Pears ●
Pomegranates ● Sharon fruit

Roasted Aubergines with Cashew and Chilli Dressing

Cost: £2.61
Serves 4

This richly-flavoured starter is best served warm or at room temperature. If you have to store it in the fridge, don't forget to take it out a couple of hours before serving.

**2 small aubergines, about 225 g (8 oz) each
olive oil, for brushing
1 fat fresh red or green chilli
50 g (2 oz) cashew nuts
25 g (1 oz) fresh coriander, trimmed and roughly chopped
175 ml (6 fl oz) Greek yogurt
salt and freshly ground black pepper
½ small green pepper, deseeded and finely diced
coarsely chopped roasted cashew nuts, to garnish**

1 Cut the aubergines in half lengthways. With cut sides down, cut lengthways again into 6 mm (¼ in) slices. Brush lightly with oil on both sides and arrange in a single layer in a roasting tin. Roast in a preheated oven at 220°C/425°F/ Gas 7 for 15-20 minutes, turning occasionally, until golden.

2 Add the chilli to the roasting tin and roast for 10 minutes until the skin is blistered and beginning to blacken. Peel off the skin, discard the seeds and roughly chop the flesh.

3 Put the cashew nuts in a small roasting tin and put in the oven for 3-5 minutes until golden. Then put them in a blender and process until very finely chopped. Add the chilli, coriander, yogurt, and salt and pepper, and purée until smooth.

4 Arrange the aubergine slices attractively on individual plates. Spoon over some of the dressing, sprinkle with the green pepper and garnish with chopped cashews.

Grilled Oriental Chicken Wings with Egg Noodles

Cost: £2.65
Serves 4

Snap up bargain packs of chicken wings and use them for relaxed entertaining. They're so finger lickin' good that knives and forks are out of the question!

**5 tbsp tomato ketchup
2 tbsp hoisin sauce
1 tbsp soy sauce
1 tbsp sugar
1 tbsp wine vinegar
1 tbsp Worcestershire sauce
8 chicken wings
oil, for brushing**

**EGG NOODLES
250 g (9 oz) medium egg noodles
2 tbsp groundnut oil
1 garlic clove, finely chopped
1 fresh chilli, deseeded and sliced
1.5 cm (¾ in) piece fresh ginger root, finely chopped
4 spring onions, sliced diagonally
2 tsp soy sauce
1 tsp toasted sesame oil
salt and freshly ground black pepper**

1 Combine the ketchup, hoisin sauce, soy sauce, sugar, wine vinegar and Worcestershire sauce. Pour the mixture over the chicken wings, making sure they are well-coated. Cover and leave to marinate in the fridge for at least 2 hours or overnight. Allow to come to room temperature before grilling.

2 Arrange the wings in a single layer on a rack in a grill pan. Place under a preheated hot grill about 17.5 cm (6 in) from the heat source for 20-25 minutes, turning regularly, until the flesh is no longer pink and the skin is slightly blackened.

3 Meanwhile, cook the noodles according to the packet instructions, then drain thoroughly.

4 Heat the oil in a wok or large frying pan until very hot. Add the garlic, chilli, ginger and spring onions, and stir-fry for 30 seconds. Remove from the pan and set aside.

5 Add the noodles to the pan and stir-fry over a high heat until heated through. Stir in the garlic mixture and sprinkle with the soy sauce and sesame oil. Season to taste and serve at once with the chicken wings.

Baked Bananas with Tangerine and Cardamom Cream

Cost: £1.72
Serves 4

You can use any loose-skinned citrus fruit instead of tangerines. If you don't have cardamom seeds, leave them out, or try another sweet spice such as crushed star anise, freshly grated nutmeg or ground cinnamon.

2 tbsp fine-cut marmalade
2 tbsp lemon juice
6 tbsp tangerine juice
4 bananas
seeds from 8 cardamom pods, crushed
150 ml (¼ pt) whipping
cream, whipped

1 Melt the marmalade in a small saucepan. Remove from the heat and mix with the lemon juice and half the tangerine juice.

2 Peel and slice the bananas lengthways and lay them in a shallow baking dish. Add the marmalade mixture and half the cardamom seeds. Bake in a preheated oven at 220°C/ 425°F/Gas 7 for 15-20 minutes, until bubbling.

3 Whip the cream until stiff, then stir in the remaining tangerine juice.

4 Arrange the bananas on individual plates and pour over the juices. Top with a spoonful of cream and sprinkle with the remaining cardamom seeds.

NUTRITIONAL INFORMATION

First course per portion: calories 170 ●
protein 6g ● fat 14g ●
carbohydrate 6g ● fibre 3g ●
source of: fibre, B vitamins

Main course per portion: calories 440 ●
protein 23g ● fat 15g ●
carbohydrate 57g ● fibre 2g ●
source of: iron, zinc,
B group vitamins

Dessert per portion: calories 255 ●
protein 2g ● fat 14g ●
carbohydrate 31g ● fibre 1g ●
source of: vitamins B6, C

2 Put the oil, butter, chilli flakes and coriander seeds in a large saucepan and heat gently for a few seconds to flavour the oil.
3 Add the onion and celery, then cover and cook over a medium heat for 5-7 minutes until softened. Add the pumpkin and all but 2 tbsp of the peanuts. Cover and cook for another 5 minutes.
4 Pour in the stock and tomatoes, and bring to the boil. Cover and simmer over a low heat for about 30 minutes.
5 Purée in a blender, then push through a sieve, pressing with the back of a wooden spoon to extract all the liquid.
6 Reheat gently and season to taste with salt and pepper. Swirl a little soured cream or yogurt into each serving and garnish with the reserved peanuts, roughly chopped.

Pumpkin and Peanut Soup

Cost: £1.28
Serves 4

Peanuts give this rich hearty soup an enigmatic flavour.

100 g (4 oz) unsalted peanuts
1 tbsp vegetable oil
25 g (1 oz) butter
pinch of dried chilli flakes
1 tsp coriander seeds, crushed
1 onion, chopped
2 celery sticks, chopped
600 g (1¼ lb) pumpkin, peeled,
deseeded and diced
850 ml (1½ pt) stock
200 g (7 oz) can chopped tomatoes
salt and freshly ground
black pepper
2 tbsp soured cream or
plain yogurt

1 Spread out the peanuts in a small roasting tin and roast in a preheated oven at 180°C/350°F/Gas 4 for 7-10 minutes until golden. If the nuts have skins, rub them off with a clean, dry tea towel.

Spiced Chicken and Green Bean Risotto

Cost: £3.10
Serves 4

For perfect results, keep the stock simmering in a small saucepan over a gentle heat. The finished risotto should be creamy and moist but not runny. Serve with buttered kale or cabbage.

450 g (1 lb) frozen chicken breasts,
defrosted
100 g (4 oz) green beans
4 tbsp vegetable oil
40 g (1½ oz) butter
50 g (2 oz) finely chopped onion
1 fresh green chilli, deseeded
and finely chopped
1 large garlic clove, finely chopped
3 thin slices fresh ginger root,
finely chopped
275 g (10 oz) arborio rice
1 L (1¾ pt) hot chicken stock
4 tbsp chopped fresh coriander
2 tbsp freshly grated Parmesan
cheese
salt and freshly ground
black pepper

1 Remove the skin and bones from the chicken. Cut the flesh into 6 mm (¼ in) x 4 cm (1½ in) strips.

2 Plunge the beans into plenty of boiling water. Boil for 1 minute, then drain and chop into 2.5 cm (1 in) pieces.

3 Heat the oil and 15 g (½ oz) of the butter in a large frying pan. Add the chicken and fry for 5 minutes. Add the onion, chilli, garlic and ginger, and gently fry for a few more minutes until the onion is soft.

4 Add the rice, stirring until the grains are glistening and coated with oil. Pour in 300 ml (½ pt) of hot stock. Simmer over a medium heat, stirring constantly until the liquid has been absorbed. Add another 150 ml (¼ pt) of stock and stir again until absorbed. Continue in this way for about 25-30 minutes, gradually adding the stock and stirring until the rice is tender but still firm to bite.

5 Stir in the beans, coriander, Parmesan and remaining butter, and season to taste.

Sharon Fruit Ginger Cream

Cost: £2.03
Serves 4

Sharon fruit look similar to persimmons, but you can eat the skin and they do not set your teeth on edge in the same way. Their orange, jelly-like flesh is absolutely delicious and packed with carotene and vitamin C. At around 38p each, Sharon fruit are not particularly cheap, but there is no reason why frugal feasters should miss out on their short season. A ripe Sharon fruit looks almost swollen but feels soft, and may have brown spots on the skin.

3 ripe Sharon fruit
2.5 cm (1 in) piece fresh ginger root
150 ml (¼ pt) double cream
2 tbsp sugar, or to taste
150 ml (¼ pt) Greek yogurt

1 Using a very sharp knife, cut two thin horizontal slices across the widest part of one of the Sharon fruits; cut in half and set aside for decoration.

2 Using a teaspoon, scoop the flesh from the remaining fruit into a bowl. Peel the ginger and put in a garlic press. Squeeze out the juice and add to the Sharon fruit. Purée the mixture in a blender until smooth.

3 Whip the cream until stiff, then fold in the sugar and yogurt. Swirl in the purée. Divide the mixture between four small serving bowls.

4 Chill until ready to serve. Decorate with the reserved Sharon fruit slices.

NUTRITIONAL INFORMATION

First course per portion: calories 260 ● protein 9g ● fat 20g ● carbohydrate 12g ● fibre 4g ● source of: calcium, iron, zinc, iodine, vitamins A, B, B6, C, E, folate

Main course per portion: calories 590 ● protein 33g ● fat 28g ● carbohydrate 56g ● fibre 1g ● source of: calcium, iron, zinc, iodine, vitamins A, B group, C

Dessert per portion: calories 305 ● protein 4g ● fat 21g ● carbohydrate 26g ● fibre 1g ● source of: beta-carotene, vitamin C

1½ tbsp lime juice
125 ml (4 fl oz) Greek yogurt
2 tbsp double cream
salt and freshly ground black pepper

MENU 3
Vegetarian
Total cost £4.41

•

Oven-Baked Tomatoes with Coriander Cream

•

White Root Gratin

•

Orange and Pomegranate Salad

1½ tbsp lime juice
125 ml (4 fl oz) Greek yogurt
2 tbsp double cream
salt and freshly ground black pepper

1 Pack the tomatoes in a single layer in a shallow ovenproof dish. Sprinkle with the olive oil, salt, pepper, sugar and coriander seeds. Bake in a preheated oven at 150°C/300°F/ Gas 2 for 2 hours.

2 Put the coriander, spring onions, garlic and lime juice in a blender. Purée for 3 minutes, frequently scraping the side of the goblet. Pour the mixture into a bowl, stir in the yogurt and cream, and season to taste.

3 Arrange the tomatoes on individual plates, garnish with a few olives and add a dollop of coriander cream.

White Root Gratin

Cost: £1.34
Serves 4

Be adventurous with your choice of root vegetables: try mixing celeriac, Jerusalem artichokes or kohlrabi with parsnips and potatoes.

1 tbsp vegetable oil
1 small onion, finely chopped
2 garlic cloves, finely chopped
400 g (14 oz) can chopped tomatoes
3 tbsp chopped fresh parsley
1 tbsp finely chopped fresh rosemary
salt and freshly ground black pepper
450 g (1 lb) peeled white root
vegetables, cut into 6 mm (¼ in) slices
cayenne pepper
50 g (2 oz) Cheddar cheese, grated

1 Heat the oil in a frying pan and gently fry the onion for 5 minutes until soft but not coloured. Add the garlic and fry for another minute.

2 Stir in the tomatoes, parsley, half the rosemary, and salt and pepper to taste. Simmer gently for 5-8 minutes until slightly reduced and thickened.

3 Meanwhile, put all the root vegetables in a steamer basket and steam over boiling water for 5 minutes until only just tender.

Oven-Baked Tomatoes with Coriander Cream

Cost: £1.29
Serves 4

Slow baking really intensifies the flavour of tomatoes – even boring winter ones will be transformed. If you can't get hold of a cheap, big bunch of coriander from a market or ethnic shop, use a mixture of parsley and coriander instead. Serve warm or at room temperature, with crusty bread.

6 large tomatoes, halved horizontally
3 tbsp olive oil
coarse sea salt
freshly ground black pepper
1 tsp muscovado sugar
crushed coriander seeds
pitted black olives, to garnish

CORIANDER CREAM

75 g (3 oz) fresh coriander
(or a mixture of coriander and
parsley), trimmed and roughly
chopped
2 spring onions, chopped
1 garlic clove, crushed

4 Arrange the vegetables in layers in a lightly greased shallow ovenproof dish, seasoning each layer with the remaining rosemary, cayenne pepper to taste, and salt and pepper. Spoon the tomato mixture over the top and sprinkle with the grated cheese.

5 Cover with foil and bake in a preheated oven at 190°C/375°F/Gas 5 for 15 minutes. Remove the foil and bake for another 15 minutes until the cheese is bubbling.

Orange and Pomegranate Salad

Cost: £1.78
Serves 4

Serve this colourful and refreshing dessert well chilled.

4 large oranges
2 pomegranates
2 tbsp clear honey
pinch of cinnamon
dash of brandy or orange-flavoured liqueur

1 Peel the oranges, removing all the pith. Using a very sharp knife, cut into thin horizontal slices, reserving the juice.

2 Roll one of the pomegranates on a work surface, pressing hard with the palm of your hand to release the juice. Cut in half and squeeze the juice into a sieve placed over a small bowl. Mix with the honey and reserved orange juice.

3 Break open the second pomegranate and remove the seeds.

4 Layer the orange slices and pomegranate seeds in a serving bowl, or arrange on individual plates. Pour the juice over the fruit, sprinkle with cinnamon and a dash of brandy.

NUTRITIONAL INFORMATION

First course per portion: calories 170 ● protein 4g ● fat 14g ● carbohydrate 9g ● fibre 2g ● source of: vitamins B1, B3, B6, C

Main course per portion: calories 265 ● protein 9g ● fat 9g ● carbohydrate 38g ● fibre 8g ● source of: calcium, fibre, folate, vitamin C

Dessert per portion: calories 100 ● protein 2g ● fat trace ● carbohydrate 23g ● fibre 5g ● source of: fibre, vitamin C, folate, B group vitamins

MENU 4
Vegetarian
Total cost £6.86

●

Sesame Rice Balls with Dipping Sauce

●

Oriental Vegetable Casserole

●

Mango, Coconut and Tapioca Pudding

Sesame Rice Balls with Dipping Sauce

Cost: £1.95
Serves 4

Crisp-fried rice balls dipped in a tangy sauce make a substantial starter. For this you need rice that sticks together; a white short-grain rice is the ideal choice. Cooking the rice in more water than usual and chilling it afterwards also helps make it sticky. Serve the balls warm or at room temperature. If possible, use shoyu or tamari (Japanese soy sauce) for the sauce. It has a mellower, lighter flavour than ordinary soy sauce.

225 g (8 oz) white short-grain rice
500 ml (18 fl oz) water
1 tsp salt
75 g (3 oz) spring onions, green parts included
2 garlic cloves, very finely chopped
pinch of dried chilli flakes
2 cm (¾ in) piece fresh ginger root, very finely chopped
½ tsp freshly ground black pepper
75 g (3 oz) alfalfa sprouts
50 g (2 oz) sesame seeds

2 tbsp plain flour
groundnut oil, for deep frying
¼ Chinese cabbage, shredded
alfalfa sprouts, to garnish

DIPPING SAUCE
2 tbsp sunflower seeds
1 tbsp finely chopped fresh coriander, chives or parsley
1 tbsp soy sauce
1 tsp white wine vinegar or rice vinegar
125 ml (4 fl oz) water
few drops toasted sesame oil

1 Rinse the rice, then put in a saucepan with the water and salt. Bring to the boil, stir once, then cover tightly and cook over a very low heat for 20-25 minutes until the water is absorbed. Tip into a bowl, allow to cool, then chill.

2 Next make the sauce. Put the sunflower seeds in a small, heavy-based pan without any oil. Dry-fry for 2-3 minutes until beginning to colour. Immediately remove from the heat. Allow to cool a little, then put in a blender with the remaining sauce ingredients and purée for several minutes until smooth. Pour into a serving bowl or small individual bowls and set aside until ready to serve.

3 Next, slice the spring onions lengthways into quarters. Cut some of the green part into 2.5 cm (1 in) shreds and reserve as a garnish. Chop the remaining onions crossways into tiny pieces, and combine with the garlic, chilli, ginger and pepper. Stir this mixture into the rice, mixing well, then stir in the alfalfa sprouts.

4 With wet hands, form the mixture into 12 balls, squeezing firmly and rolling them in the palm of your hands to make them stick. They can be prepared ahead of time up to this point.

5 When ready to fry, roll each ball in the sesame seeds, then in the flour.

6 Pour about 10 cm (4 in) oil in a deep-fat fryer or saucepan and heat to 180°C (350°F) or until a cube of bread browns in 30 seconds. Fry the rice balls a few at a time, for 5-7 minutes until brown and crisp. Drain on paper towel.

7 Arrange the Chinese leaves and alfalfa sprouts on a serving plate. Place the rice balls in the middle and sprinkle with the reserved spring onion. Serve with the dipping sauce.

Oriental Vegetable Casserole

Cost: £2.92

Serves 4

The vegetables are lightly cooked so that they retain their shape. Serve with lightly steamed broccoli. Don't waste the broccoli stalks, slice them thinly and add to the casserole. They are a beautiful shape and deliciously crunchy.

1 aubergine, cut into 1 cm (½ in) slices
olive oil
1 tbsp sesame seeds
1 onion, finely chopped
2 garlic cloves, finely chopped
2 x 400 g (14 oz) cans chopped tomatoes
2 tbsp soy sauce
1 tbsp dry sherry
½ tsp sugar
salt and freshly ground black pepper
100 g (4 oz) mushrooms, thickly sliced
1 tsp coriander seeds, crushed
1 fresh chilli, deseeded and finely chopped
2 yellow peppers, deseeded and sliced
2 carrots, cut into thin diagonal slices
75 g (3 oz) broccoli stalks, thinly sliced
2 courgettes, cut into 2 cm (¾ in) diagonal slices
2 tbsp chopped fresh coriander

1 Arrange the aubergine slices in a single layer in a roasting tin. Brush with olive oil on both sides. Roast in a preheated oven at 230°C/450°F/Gas 8 for 20-25 minutes, until golden. Cut the larger pieces into quarters and set aside.
2 Put the sesame seeds in a small, heavy-based frying pan without any oil. Dry-fry for a few minutes until just beginning to darken. Immediately remove from the pan and set aside.
3 Heat 2 tbsp of the oil in a saucepan. Gently fry the onion for 5 minutes. Add the garlic and fry for 1 minute. Stir in the tomatoes, soy sauce, sherry, sugar, and salt and pepper to taste. Simmer gently, until slightly thickened.
4 Meanwhile, heat 5 tbsp of the oil in a large pan or flameproof casserole. Add the mushrooms and stir-fry over a medium heat for 5 minutes. Add the coriander seeds, chilli, yellow pepper, carrot, broccoli and courgette. Cover and cook for 5 minutes, then add the aubergine.

5 Stir in the tomato sauce. Cover and simmer for 10 minutes. Check the seasoning and stir in the sesame seeds and coriander.

Mango, Coconut and Tapioca Pudding

Cost: £1.99

Serves 4

Those put off by memories of 'frog spawn' served at school should give tapioca a second chance. It is cheap and nutritious, and makes a lovely juicy mango go a long way.

40 g (1½ oz) tapioca
400 g (14 oz) can coconut milk
1 mango, weighing about 450 g (1 lb)
2 tbsp sugar
juice and finely grated zest of 2 limes

1 Put the tapioca and coconut milk in a small saucepan. Bring to the boil, then simmer over a low heat, stirring frequently to prevent sticking, for 15-20 minutes until thickened. Leave to cool.
2 With the narrow side of the mango facing you, slice vertically down one side about 2.5 cm (1 in) away from the centre – you should just miss the stone. Repeat with the other side. Remove the peel and chop the flesh. Peel and scrape off any flesh attached to the stone.
3 Purée the flesh with the sugar and lime juice. Stir into the tapioca. Pour into individual serving bowls and sprinkle with the lime zest. Cover and chill until ready to serve.

NUTRITIONAL INFORMATION

First course per portion: calories 520 • protein 11g • fat 28g • carbohydrate 59g • fibre 3g • source of: calcium, iron, zinc, selenium, vitamins B1, B6, E

Main course per portion: calories 300 • protein 7g • fat 23g • carbohydrate 17g • fibre 6g • source of: calcium, iron, zinc, vitamins A, B1, B6, E, folate

Dessert per portion: calories 110 • protein 1g • fat 0.5g • carbohydrate 28g • fibre 1g • source of: beta-carotene, vitamin C

ACCOMPANYING VEGETABLES, SALADS AND SAUCES

Cajun Roasted Roots

Cost: 86p
Serves 4

700 g (1½ lb) mixed root vegetables,
eg potatoes, celeriac, parsnips,
Jerusalem artichokes
8 tbsp vegetable oil
½-1 tsp cajun seasoning
salt and freshly ground black
pepper

1 Peel the vegetables and steam over boiling
salted water for about 5 minutes until just
beginning to soften. Cut them into even-sized
pieces about 2 cm (¾ in) square.
2 Heat the oil in a roasting tin large enough to
take the vegetables in a single layer. When the
oil is very hot, add the vegetables. Sprinkle with
cajun seasoning, and salt and pepper, turning
well to coat.
3 Roast in a preheated oven at 220°C/425°F/
Gas 7 for about 30-40 minutes until brown and
crisp. Drain on paper towel before serving.

> **NUTRITIONAL INFORMATION**
> *Per portion:* calories 350 ● protein 3g ●
> fat 31g ● carbohydrate 18g ● fibre 5g ●
> source of: folic acid, vitamins B1, C, E

Roasted Butternut Squash

Cost: £1.33
Serves 4

1 large butternut squash
oil, for brushing
salt and freshly ground black pepper
brown sugar
snipped fresh chives to garnish

1 Cut the squash in half lengthways, remove
the seeds, then cut each half in two. Brush the
cut surfaces with oil. Season generously with
salt and pepper, and sprinkle with a little sugar.
2 Roast in the top of the oven at 180°C/350°F/
Gas 4, for about an hour, until soft. Garnish
with chives.

> **NUTRITIONAL INFORMATION**
> *Per portion:* calories 75 ● protein 1g ●
> fat 3g ● carbohydrate 11g ● fibre 2g ●
> source of: beta-carotene, vitamin C

Parsnip and Sesame Purée

Cost: 59p
Serves 4

600 g (1¼ lb) parsnips
1 tsp sesame seeds
25 g (1 oz) butter
salt and freshly ground black
pepper

1 Peel the parsnips and cut into chunks. Steam
over boiling water for about 10 minutes until just
tender.
2 Meanwhile, put the sesame seeds in a
small, heavy-based frying pan. Dry-fry
(without any oil) for a few minutes until the
aroma rises.
3 Mash the parsnips and stir in the sesame
seeds, butter, and salt and pepper. Add a little of
the water from the steamer if the mixture seems
too dry.

> **NUTRITIONAL INFORMATION**
> *Per portion:* calories 165 ● protein 3g ●
> fat 9g ● carbohydrate 19g ● fibre 7g ●
> source of: iron, folate, beta-carotene,
> vitamins C, E

New Potatoes with Mint and Cumin

Cost: 32p
Serves 4

600 g (1¼ lb) small new potatoes
1 tsp cumin seeds
knob of butter
1 tbsp chopped fresh mint
salt and freshly ground black pepper

1 Boil the potatoes in salted water until only just soft.
2 Dry-fry the cumin seeds in a small pan until you can smell their aroma.
3 Drain the potatoes, transfer to a warm dish and stir in the butter, cumin, mint and seasoning.

NUTRITIONAL INFORMATION
Per portion: calories 125 ● protein 2g ●
fat 3g ● carbohydrate 26g ● fibre 2g ●
source of: vitamin C

Garlic Potatoes

Cost: 55p
Serves 4

4 large old potatoes, unpeeled
5 tbsp extra virgin olive oil
1 garlic clove, finely chopped
2 tsp finely chopped fresh thyme
salt and freshly ground
black pepper
6 black olives, pitted and sliced
chopped parsley, to garnish

1 Cook the potatoes in boiling water until only just tender. Drain well and remove the skins. Slice the potatoes thickly and put them in a large bowl.
2 Pour the oil over the potatoes, and add the garlic and thyme. Season to taste, then gently toss the slices, taking care not to break them.
3 Overlap the slices in a shallow ovenproof dish and sprinkle with the olive slices. Drizzle over any oil from the bowl.
4 Bake in a preheated oven at 200°C/400°F/ Gas 6 for 15 minutes, until crisp. Garnish with parsley before serving.

NUTRITIONAL INFORMATION
Per portion: calories 270 ● protein 3g ●
fat 17g ● carbohydrate 27g ● fibre 2g ●
source of: vitamins B6, C

Oven-Baked Buttered Potatoes

Cost: 58p
Serves 4

900 g (2 lb) old potatoes
salt and freshly ground black
pepper
75 g (3 oz) butter
125 ml (4 fl oz) milk

1 Using a very sharp knife or, better still, a mandoline, cut the potatoes into 3 mm (⅛ in) slices. Rinse off the starch under running water, then pat dry with paper towel.
2 Butter a shallow baking dish then arrange a layer of overlapping potato slices in the bottom. Season with salt and pepper and dot with butter. Continue in this way until all the slices have been used up. Make sure the final layer is generously dotted with butter. Pour in the milk.
3 Bake in a preheated oven at 200°C/400°F/ Gas 6 for 50-60 minutes until the top is brown and crispy.

NUTRITIONAL INFORMATION
Per portion: calories 320 ● protein 6g ●
fat 16g ● carbohydrate 40g ● fibre 3g ●
source of: iodine, vitamins A, B group, C

Courgette and Carrot Ribbons

Cost: 83p
Serves 4

3 courgettes
3 carrots
knob of butter
1 tsp finely chopped fresh rosemary
salt and freshly ground black pepper

1 Using a swivel peeler, shave the courgettes and carrots into wide ribbons, working from opposite sides towards the centre.
2 Place in a steamer basket over boiling water for 4-5 minutes until only just tender.
3 Transfer to a warm serving dish and stir in the butter, rosemary and seasoning.

Spicy Greens

Cost: 46p
Serves 4

350 g (12 oz) spring greens or
green cabbage
2 tbsp groundnut oil
1 tsp mustard seeds
2 slices fresh ginger root,
finely chopped
1 garlic clove, finely chopped
¼ tsp dried chilli flakes
3 tbsp water or stock

1 Remove and discard any tough stalks from
the greens. Stack the leaves and slice crossways
into thin ribbons.
2 Heat the oil in a large pan until almost
smoking. Add the mustard seeds and fry until
they start to pop. Stir in the greens, ginger,
garlic and chilli flakes. Stir-fry for 1 minute.
3 Lower the heat and add the water or stock.
Cover and cook for 3-5 minutes, stirring
occasionally, until the greens are tender but still
crisp and brightly coloured.

Spinach Purée with Red Pepper

Cost: £1.06
Serves 4

800 g (1¾ lb) spinach
3 tbsp vegetable oil
1 small onion, finely chopped
1 small red pepper, deseeded and diced
salt and freshly ground black pepper

1 Remove the stalks from the spinach and
wash the leaves in several changes of water.
Stack the leaves and slice into ribbons.
2 Put the spinach in a large saucepan without
any extra water. Cover and cook over a medium
heat for 7-10 minutes until wilted and soft.
Drain in a sieve, pressing out as much water as
possible with the back of a wooden spoon.
3 Heat the oil in a frying pan. Add the onion
and gently fry for 4-5 minutes until soft but not
coloured. Add the red pepper and fry for
another 2 minutes.
4 Add the cooked spinach and stir until heated
through. Season to taste with salt and pepper.
Serve at once.

Stir-Fried Brussels Sprouts

Cost: 85p
Serves 4

40 g (1½ oz) butter or sunflower
margarine
450 g (1 lb) Brussels sprouts,
trimmed and finely shredded
2 tbsp toasted sunflower seeds
salt and freshly ground black pepper
chopped parsley, to garnish

1 Melt the butter in a frying pan until foaming.
Add the Brussels sprouts and stir-fry over a
medium heat for 4-5 minutes until crunchy
tender but still brightly coloured.
2 Stir in the sunflower seeds, and salt and
pepper. Sprinkle with parsley and serve at
once.

Sautéed Leeks

Cost: 79p
Serves 4

This is a very quick way of cooking leeks. They are part-sautéed and part-steamed in their own juices, and remain crisp and brightly coloured.

**450 g (1 lb) leeks
knob of butter
coarse sea salt and freshly ground
black pepper
2 tbsp chopped fresh parsley**

1 Trim the leeks and slice crossways into 1 cm (½ in) pieces. Heat a large knob of butter in a heavy-based saucepan. When foaming, add the leeks with some sea salt and a few grindings of black pepper. Cover tightly and cook over a medium heat for 3-5 minutes until the leeks are tender-crisp, shaking the pan from time to time to prevent sticking.
2 Sprinkle with parsley and serve at once.

NUTRITIONAL INFORMATION
Per portion: calories 60 ● protein 2g ●
fat 5g ● carbohydrate 3g ● fibre 2g ●
source of: iron, folate, vitamins A, C, E

Roasted Leeks

Cost: 90p
Serves 4

**4 large leeks, trimmed and halved
lengthways
1 garlic clove, finely chopped
50 ml (2 fl oz) extra virgin olive oil
coarse sea salt and freshly ground
black pepper
2 tbsp chopped flat-leafed parsley**

1 Pack the leeks in a single layer in a shallow ovenproof dish. Sprinkle with the garlic, olive oil, seasoning and half the parsley, turning to coat.
2 Place in the top of the oven, preheated to 240°C/425°F/Gas 9, for 10 minutes. Turn and roast for another 10 minutes until beginning to blacken.
3 Sprinkle with the remaining parsley and a little more sea salt before serving.

NUTRITIONAL INFORMATION
Per portion: calories 120 ● protein 1g ●
fat 12g ● carbohydrate 3g ● fibre 2g ●
source of: thiamin, vitamins B6, C

Mushrooms and Green Beans with Coriander

Cost: £1.70
Serves 4

**225 g (8 oz) green beans, trimmed
4 tbsp olive oil
1 bay leaf
1 tsp coriander seeds, crushed
225 g (8 oz) button mushrooms, sliced
1 garlic clove, finely chopped
juice of 1 lemon
2 tbsp chopped fresh parsley
salt and freshly ground black pepper**

1 Plunge the beans into plenty of boiling salted water for 3 minutes. Drain, chop into 2 cm (¾ in) pieces and set aside.
2 Heat the oil in a frying pan with the bay leaf and coriander seeds. Add the mushrooms and stir-fry over a medium-high heat for about 5 minutes until most of the liquid has evaporated.
3 Stir in the garlic, lemon juice, parsley and seasoning. Fry for another 1 minute, then stir in the beans and heat through.

NUTRITIONAL INFORMATION
Per portion: calories 120 ● protein 2g ●
fat 12g ● carbohydrate 3g ● fibre 2g ●
source of: folate, vitamin C

Roasted Mushrooms

Cost: £1.53
Serves 4

**4 large flat cap mushrooms
olive oil
soy sauce
1 tsp chopped fresh marjoram
or thyme
salt and freshly ground black pepper**

1 Wipe the mushrooms clean, then place skin-side down in a greased shallow baking dish. Drizzle generously with olive oil and a little soy sauce. Sprinkle with the marjoram and season.
2 Roast in a preheated oven at 180°C/350°F/Gas 4 for 40 minutes. Add a little boiling water or stock if they seem dry.

Fennel and Tomato Salad

Cost: £1.51
Serves 4

2 fennel bulbs, quartered lengthways,
cored and sliced vertically into
very thin slivers
4 plum tomatoes with a good flavour,
cut lengthways into thin segments
3 tbsp extra virgin olive oil
squeeze of lemon juice
coarse sea salt and freshly ground
black pepper
chopped fennel fronds or parsley,
to garnish

1 Arrange the fennel and tomatoes in a serving dish or on individual plates.
2 Drizzle with the olive oil, then sprinkle with lemon juice and season to taste. Garnish with fennel fronds and serve at once.

Tomato and Basil Salad

Cost: 51p
Serves 4

350 g (12 oz) small tomatoes, quartered
pinch of sugar
salt and freshly ground black pepper
a few torn basil leaves
1 tbsp extra virgin olive oil

1 Put the tomatoes in a dish and sprinkle with sugar, and salt and pepper.
2 Add the basil leaves and the olive oil, mixing well. Leave to stand for 1 hour before serving.

Green Rice Salad

Cost: 81p
Serves 4

This needs herbs with a lively flavour. Sorrel is very easy to grow, even in a pot on the window sill. It has a sharp lemony flavour. Young dandelion leaves are free for the asking, but gather them away from roads. If you can't buy coriander cheaply from ethnic shops, use parsley or more of the other herbs.

150 g (5 oz) white rice
½ tsp salt
3 tbsp extra virgin olive oil
2 tsp white wine vinegar
finely grated zest of ½ lime
freshly ground black pepper
2 spring onions, green parts
included, chopped
50 g (2 oz) cooked peas
50 g (2 oz) cooked green beans,
chopped
2 tbsp chopped fresh coriander
1 tbsp chopped fresh mint
1 tbsp chopped fresh sorrel or
young dandelion leaves

1 Wash the rice in several changes of water until the water runs clear. Put in a small saucepan with the salt and enough water to cover by the depth of your thumbnail. Bring to the boil, covered, then simmer over a very low heat for 15 minutes until the water has been absorbed.
2 Transfer the rice to a salad bowl and fluff with a fork. Gently stir in the olive oil, wine vinegar, lime zest and pepper to taste.

3 When cool, stir in the remaining ingredients. Leave to stand at room temperature for 1-2 hours before serving.

Garden Salad

Cost: £1.72
Serves 4

Use a mixture of whatever leaves you can lay your hands on, ideally free from your garden.

**8 handfuls mixed green leaves, such as young spinach, butterhead lettuce, Little Gem lettuce, red oak lettuce, cos lettuce, lamb's lettuce or rocket
10 radishes, sliced
2 plum tomatoes, deseeded and cut into slivers
1 tbsp snipped chives
walnut oil
lemon juice or balsamic vinegar
salt and freshly ground black pepper**

1 Wash and dry the leaves and put in a serving bowl with the radishes, tomatoes and chives.
2 Toss in just enough oil to coat the leaves, then sprinkle with a dash of lemon juice or balsamic vinegar, and season to taste.

Watercress Sauce

Cost: 50p
Makes 150 ml (¼ pt)

**125 ml (4 fl oz) plain yogurt
6 tbsp chopped watercress
1 tsp wine vinegar
salt and freshly ground black pepper**

1 Combine all the ingredients in a small bowl.
2 Leave to stand for 1 hour before serving.

Minted Yogurt and Cucumber Sauce

Cost: 58p
Serves 4

**½ cucumber
salt
225 ml (8 fl oz) plain yogurt
2 tbsp chopped fresh mint
freshly ground black pepper**

1 Peel the cucumber, slice lengthways into eighths, remove seeds and chop the flesh finely.
2 Put in a colander, sprinkle with salt and toss. Leave to drain for 30 minutes, then pat dry with paper towel.
3 Mix the yogurt with the mint and pepper, then stir in the cucumber.

Grilled Tomato Sauce

Cost: 47p
Makes about 350 ml (12 fl oz)

This freezes well, so it is worth making in large quantities when tomatoes are in glut. If you prefer a smoother sauce, push it through a sieve before serving.

**400 g (14 oz) tomatoes
2 garlic cloves, unpeeled
1 tsp dried oregano
1 tbsp olive oil**

½ small onion, chopped very finely
pinch of dried chilli flakes
¼ tsp sugar
¼ tsp salt
freshly ground black pepper
knob of butter

1 Place the tomatoes and garlic under a very hot grill, turning frequently until the skins blister and blacken. The garlic will need about 10 minutes, and the tomatoes 15-20 minutes. Peel the garlic but do not peel the tomatoes.
2 Dry-fry the oregano in a small, heavy-based pan, until you smell the aroma.
3 Heat the oil in a small pan and gently fry the onion until translucent. Add the oregano and chilli flakes, and fry for another minute.
4 Put the tomatoes (including any blackened bits of skin), garlic and onion mixture in a blender and purée until smooth.
5 Pour into a frying pan and season with sugar, salt and pepper. Simmer until slightly thickened, then stir in the butter.

> **NUTRITIONAL INFORMATION**
> *Per portion:* calories 70 ● protein 1g ●
> fat 5g ● carbohydrate 5g ● fibre 1g ●
> source of: vitamins A, C, E

Quick Tomato Sauce

Cost: 33p
Makes 225 ml (8 fl oz)

3 tbsp olive oil
400 g (14 oz) can chopped tomatoes
1 tsp dried oregano
pinch of sugar
salt and freshly ground black pepper

1 Put all the ingredients in a saucepan and bring to the boil.

2 Simmer briskly for 20-25 minutes, stirring now and then, until very thick.

> **NUTRITIONAL INFORMATION**
> *Per portion:* calories 95 ● protein 1g ●
> fat 8g ● carbohydrate 4g ● fibre 1g ●
> source of: vitamins A, C, E

Green Peppercorn Sauce

Cost: 60p
Makes 300 ml (½ pt)

25 g (1 oz) butter
25 g (1 oz) flour
225 ml (8 fl oz) milk
125 ml (4 fl oz) vegetable cooking water
or additional milk
½ tsp crushed green peppercorns
2 tbsp chopped fresh coriander
or parsley
1 tbsp freshly grated Parmesan cheese
juice of ½ lemon
salt

1 Melt the butter in a small saucepan. Add the flour and stir briskly over a medium heat for about a minute.
2 Pour in the milk and water, whisking until smooth. Add the green peppercorns, then stir until just boiling. Simmer for 2-3 minutes, continuing to stir.
3 Add the coriander or parsley, Parmesan cheese, lemon juice and salt to taste. Simmer for another minute.

> **NUTRITIONAL INFORMATION**
> *Per portion:* calories 110 ● protein 4g ●
> fat 7g ● carbohydrate 7g ● fibre 0g ●
> source of: calcium, iodine

INDEX OF RECIPES